# Fishing B.C. Rivers

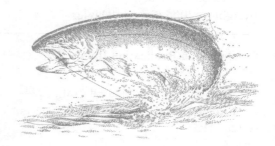

# Fishing B.C. Rivers
## Big Fish and Accessible Waterways

**Gordon Davies**

hancock
house

ISBN 0-88839-531-0

**Cataloging in Publication Data**

Davies, Gordon E. (Gordon Edward), 1924–
    Fishing B.C. rivers : big fish and accessible waterways /
Gordon Davies.

Includes index.
ISBN 0-88839-531-0

    1. Fishing—Brisitsh Columbia—Guidebooks. 2. British
Columbia—Guidebooks. I. Title.

SH572.B8D37 2004    799.1'1'09711    C2004-903039-6

Printed in China—JADE

Editing: Yvonne Lund
Production: Irene Hannestead, Ingrid Luters
Cover Design: Rick Groenheyde

*We acknowledge the financial support of the Government of Canada through the
Book Publishing Industry Development Program (BPIDP) for our publishing activities.*

Published simultaneously in Canada and the United States by

**HANCOCK HOUSE PUBLISHERS LTD.**
19313 Zero Avenue, Surrey, B.C. V3S 9R9
(604) 538-1114  Fax (604) 538-2262

**HANCOCK HOUSE PUBLISHERS**
1431 Harrison Avenue, Blaine, WA 98230-5005
(604) 538-1114  Fax (604) 538-2262
*Web Site:* www.hancockhouse.com  *email:* sales@hancockhouse.com

# Contents

# DEDICATION

This volume is dedicated to all men, women, boys and girls who would rather fish than eat.

A special "thank you" to the hundreds of people who have provided historical, geographical and personal information and photos for these humble river portraits.

My deepest gratitude to Pauline, Kay, Ann, Clint and Rob for their invaluable assistance.

*There are many pleasures to be derived by drawing up
to a comfortable rock or well-appointed stump
and watching a stream go by.*

*The soothing effects associated with water in any form
take the edges off the annoyances of daily life.*

— NORMAN STRUNG in Field & Stream

## Gordon Davies

Born in the Royal Columbian Hospital in New Westminster, BC in June, 1924, Gordon Davies says that an hour after his birth he opened his eyes, glanced out the window at the big Fraser River and said "It looks like a person could catch trout and salmon from those sandbars."

Today, still drowning worms in rivers from the Yukon Territory to British Columbia, Washington and Oregon, California and western Mexico, this incurable river angler continues to fish, explore, photograph and fall into rivers throughout the west.

During his working career, Gordon was a journeyman printing pressman and an owner-manager of a commercial printing shop, and later a journeyman compositor in daily and weekly newspapers. He has also been a freelance angling writer in magazines and newspapers in Canada, the USA and in three English-language publications in Baja California, Mexico.

# TOURISM BRITISH COLUMBIA REGIONS

**1** Northern British Columbia

**2** Thompson Okanagan

**3** Kootenay Rockies

**4** Vancouver, Coast & Mountains

**5** Cariboo Chilcotin Coast

**6** Vancouver Island

# FISHING LICENCES AND FISHING REGULATIONS

River fishing in British Columbia is regulated by the provincial government, with one exception: salmon fishing is regulated by the federal government.

Freshwater licences are available from 1500 vendors and 58 Government Agents' offices throughout the province. Many vendors are fishing tackle shops or fishing guides' offices. Either of these can provide invaluable firsthand angling advice, tackle tips and other useful information. A complete list of vendors, including some outside the province, is on the B.C. Fisheries web site.

Go to the BC Fisheries web site: www.bcfisheries.gov.bc.ca and click on "Angling Licence Vendors and Government Agents" under the Popular Topics section.

For information on the salmon fishing regulations, contact:
The office of the Chief of Recreational Fisheries, DFO.
Phone (604) 666-6331. Or go to the DFO's web site:
www.pac.dfo-mpo.gc.ca

For information on recent openings, closures or other changes in regulations, go to the BC Fisheries web site at
www.bcfisheries.gov.bc.ca,
scroll down to "In-Season Freshwater Regulation Changes and Synopsis Corrections" and click on appropriate region.

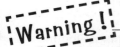

NOTE that lead is now banned in British Columbia as a material in all sinkers, lures and other terminal tackle.

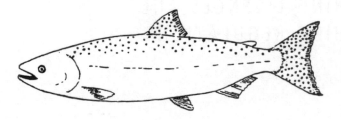

## Chinook Salmon

Aliases: Spring Salmon, King Salmon, Blackmouth, Quinnat, Tyee. The Chinook has a silvery-blue body and a silvery tail with black spots from top to bottom. Its gums are black. Maximum recorded size: 126pounds (57 kg.)

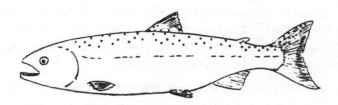

## Coho Salmon

Aliases: Silver Salmon. the high jumping, battling Coho can be counted on to give an angler plenty of action. The Coho has black spots on its back and on the upper half of its tail. The Coho's bright red flesh has a rich flavour. Maximum recorded size is 30 pounds (14kg.) but, normally, a seven-to-eleven-pounder is considered large.

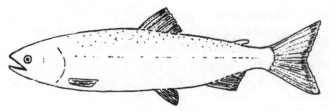

## Sockeye Salmon

Slimiest of all Pacific Salmon, the silvery-blue, almost-toothless Sockeye usually weighs 3 to 6 pounds (1.3 to 2.6 kg.) There are no distinct black markings on the body of this extremely important commercial food fish.

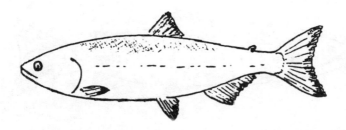

## Chum Salmon

Alias Keta or Dog Salmon. Of all Salmon, the Chum (with its high oil content) is considered the finest for smoking, and makes the best lox, according to experts. In fresh water on their spawning run, the Chums quickly develop ugly black bars on the sides of their bodies, then their flesh turns pale and almost tasteless. At this point the meat is unfit for smoking or eating. Maximum recorded weight is 33 pounds (15 kg.). More commonly they weigh between 4 and 13 pounds.

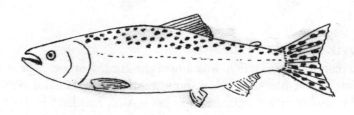

## Pink Salmon

Also known as Humpback or Humpy. Although often rated low as a table fish, the meat of the Pink Salmon, when handled properly and cooked promptly, is quite tasty whether fried, baked, broiled or used for fish and chips or a salmon souffle. This salmon is easily identified by the large, oval spots on its entire tail. Spots on its back are also quite big. Maximum recorded size is 15 pounds (6.8 kg.).

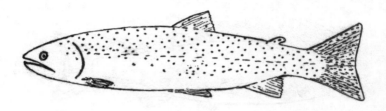

## Cutthroat Trout

The Cutthroat Trout is found throughout most of B.C. in lakes, rivers, creeks and in the waters of the ocean. They have heavy spotting, and red slashes (may be faint) on the lower jaw. Cutthroat weighing over 40 pounds have been caught by anglers.

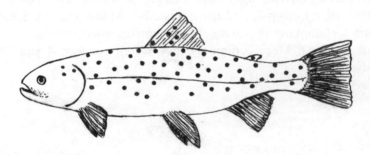

## Brown Trout

This exceptional gamefish was imported from Europe a century ago. Fairly large black or brown spots, many with light halos. World record is 39 pounds, 8 ounces, from Loch Awe, Scotland in 1866.

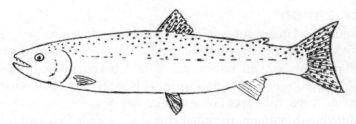

## Steelhead

The Steelhead is an ocean-going race of rainbow trout. No teeth at back of tongue. No red slashes under lower jaw. Maximum recorded size is 45 inches (114 cm.) 43 pounds (19.5 kg.).

# IDENTIFICATION OF SPECIES

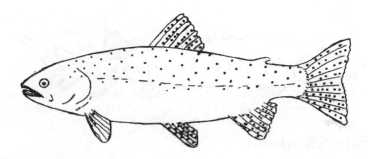

## Rainbow Trout

Small black spots, mostly restricted to above the lateral line. Radiating rows of spots on tail. 40 pounders have been caught by anglers.

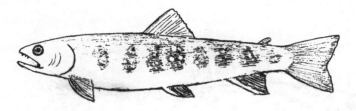

## Dolly Varden Char

Aliases: Bull Trout, Brook Char, Sea Char. The Dolly is distributed all over B.C. Usually weighs from 2 to 10 pounds. World record is 40 pounds (18 kg.).

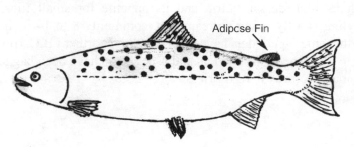

Adipose Fin

## Adipose Fin

The Adipose fin is a small fleshy appendage common to all Trout, Salmon and Char. Fish hatchery personnel often clip off the adipose fins of young salmonids for purposes of identification.

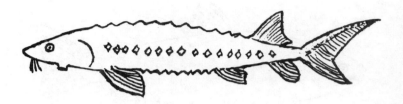

## White Sturgeon

These remarkable fish have existed on earth since the days of the dinosaurs. The well-armored critters have many large, bony scales along their backs and sides. British Columbia, in its lower reaches, has the finest sturgeon fishery in North America. The largest specimen on record was 20 feet long and weighed 1,800 pounds (816 kilos).

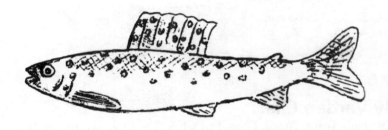

## Arctic Grayling

With its high dorsal sailfin and its appetite for small flies, the Grayling is a fly caster's dream fish. commonly 8 to 14 inches in length, some 3-pounders have been caught in northern B.C. (only in Arctic watershed). 4-pounders and 5-pounders have been bagged in Canada's Northwest Territories.

## Walleye

Its nickname in Northern B.C. and Alberta, "Pickerel", is a total misnomer. This fish is a moderately good fighter, but its greatest attribute is the fine flavour of its flesh when cooked.

## Mountain Whitefish

Erroneously called "grayling" in some areas, the little mountain whitefish is caught on live maggots, bottled single salmon eggs, garden worms, dry flies and wet flies. These are rather small fish (6 to 12 inches in length), but occasionally a 13-to16-incher is caught.

## Pike

Alias Jackfish, Snake, Northern, Jack and—for skinny immature Pikes—Hammer Handle. In B.C. Pike are present in the Peace River watershed and in most river systems farther north. World record is 46 pounds, 2 ounces, from Sacandaga Reservoir, New York State, in 1940.

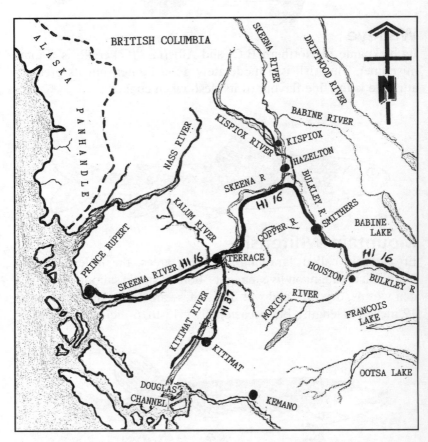

**Northern region of British Columbia — southwest section**

# CHAPTER 1

# The Giant Salmon of Kitimat
plus the Kalum River

*The Kitimat is an exceptional steelhead river. I have a life-long
love of this river and an enormous passion for steelheading. Like
most steelheaders, I have no problem putting live fish back exactly where I got them from. It is ironic, however, that most of us
male anglers have a problem putting things back where we got
them from in the kitchen... (Just ask my wife.)*

— RON WAKITA, Fishing Guide and Master River Fisherman

**K**itimat fisherman Carlos Furtado beached a gigantic seventy-
eight-pound chinook salmon at Coho Flats on the Kitimat
River in 1988. On the Kitimat in 1989, local angler Shawn
Alderman caught a sixty-seven pounder and Alois Huber nailed a
sixty-five-pound chinook. In the same year Robert Gardner of
Horsefly, BC, took a seventy-two-pound giant from the lower river.
In 1999, Kitimat angler Darrel Little subdued a sixty-five-pounder
with rather light tackle that was more suitable for playing a ten-
pound coho salmon than a lunker chinook. He hooked the big fish
above the Haisla Bridge (almost in the middle of town) then spent
most of the next half-hour looking at an empty spool and watching
the heavy salmon performing cartwheels. He had the fish on the
beach in thirty minutes-but he confessed, "I got lucky."

Don't be so modest, Darrel!

In July the Kitimat River certainly produces an incredible number of humungous chinook salmon (alias spring, king, tyee, black-

Darrel Little of Kitimat, B.C. caught this 65-pound Chinook, June 8 1999.
*Photo: Reliable Guide & Charter*

mouth, smiley and quinnat). The great river's incredible trophy salmon fishing has created an almost carnival-like atmosphere—frenzied and frantic at times—as hundreds of anglers from the USA and Europe move into the small community of Kitimat on the northern coast of British Columbia, and camp along the riverbank. Although excellent pools are easy to reach by road, visitors can learn everything about this great river from Ron Wakita and his staff at the fishing tackle department of his Home Hardware store at 380 City Center, Kitimat. Phone (250) 632-3522.

The fabulous runs of big chinooks owe their existence today to the continued hard work of the Kitimat River Fish Hatchery. The facility began full-scale operations in 1983, just barely in time to be able to save dwindling stocks of salmon and steelhead seriously depleted by industrial pollution, by shortsighted and ruinous logging practices, and by angling pressure.

Human beings may have established industries and built a small city on the river, but the valley's fauna and flora remain surprisingly wild and undomesticated. Here indeed is a scenic wonderland, in spite of modern man's urbanization and industrialization. When you visit a northern British Columbia community, you are seldom far from the primeval forest and the beasts of the bush. This is particularly evident in late summer near Kitimat when black bears are seen strolling along the riverbank, hunting salmon, completely at ease, even within the city limits.

Originating in the wild hills east of the town, the famous fishy stream heads northward, swings to the west, then passes under the Highway 37 Bridge. It makes a left turn, flows southward through downtown Kitimat, then into Douglas Channel and from the channel to the western sea. This rambling, racing river is a joy to behold—backed by majestic white-capped mountains and rich, dark green cedar and spruce forests—with maples, alders, ferns, fireweed, thimbleberries and thistles abundant along its gravelly banks.

The twenty miles of accessible water between the Highway 37 Bridge and the river mouth is the most heavily fished section of the Kitimat River. You'll find many fine pools that can be reached quite easily via roads and trails, starting at the bridge and following the river downstream. Below the highway bridge, the Log Jam Pool holds steelhead and salmon. There is also some fine steelhead water above the bridge. In the next few miles, you can find several picture-perfect fishing holes, including the Litter Barrel Pool, the Old Sawmill Pool and the Crown Bridge Pools. Continuing downriver, just before you reach the town of Kitimat, you come to two popular coho fishing hot spots—Cablecar and Coho Flats.

The little city of Kitimat was established near the river mouth in the early 1950s to accommodate employees of one of the largest aluminum manufacturing facilities in the world. The Alcan Aluminum plant now employs more than two thousand workers.

A famous landmark in Kitimat, a five-hundred-year-old Sitka spruce on the eastern shore of the river, enjoys protection under the law. British Columbia's largest living spruce tree measures thirty-seven feet in circumference and is one hundred and sixty-five feet tall. This spruce—a seedling when Columbus landed in the New World—contains enough lumber to frame ten houses, say some tree experts. At the east end of the Haisla Bridge, near the old tree, anglers can park at the Rod and Gun clubhouse and follow a trail upriver to two well-known salmon pools. Radley Park, a well maintained, reasonably priced camp for visiting anglers and vacationers, can be found on the gravel-strewn shore of the Kitimat River at the west end of the Haisla Bridge. Radley is a first-rate community-operated campground, situated on a piece of land with an ancient,

Brenda Weitman hoisting a 42-pound Chinook Salmon.

tragic history. There once was a Haisla village named Tlagachiyukwis (Place of the Thimbleberry Leaves) on the site of this present-day park. A violent freshet wiped out this entire village one long-ago autumn, flattening homes and sweeping away the villagers' canoes. The residents who managed to survive this destructive flood abandoned the site forever.

Free firewood, a huge community fish smoker and a sani-dump for recreational vehicles are some of the amenities available at Radley Park. In July when the chinook salmon are running, the camp attendants claim that over two hundred anglers are in the park every day. A two-minute drive downstream from Radley Park will take you to a very popular pool—the Pump House Hole. Across the river on the eastern shore, be sure to look for the Pump House Dike and the Island Bar.

When the river is crowded with hopeful chinook fishermen in July, it isn't surprising that some of these anglers don't succeed in landing trophy-sized salmon. The reason is obvious. In the powerful current of the lower Kitimat River, these huge salmon are anything but easy to subdue. Often, a large Kitimat chinook will mouth a lure deceptively softly, lulling the creature at the other end of the line into a false sense of security. Then, after a moment's consideration, the fish will shift into overdrive and race madly downriver. Nearly all of these chinook salmon run downstream when hooked, but some very ornery ones will head straight up the river. One late afternoon in July at the Pump House Dike, I watched a local angler battling a jumbo-sized chinook. The fisherman couldn't stop the salmon's downstream dash. He couldn't even slow it down. Fish and fisherman parted company after a very brief tug-of-war, in spite of a heavy line!

"I'm not surprised," the angler remarked philosophically. "I've always said these Kitimat chinooks are completely unpredictable, sometimes they'll tear off downstream at full speed until they spool you. But there are times when they'll actually help you beach them; like the day I was wading from the dike to the Island Bar. While I was sloshing along, I absentmindedly made one cast—and as soon as the lure hit the water, I connected with a big salmon. The fish ran straight toward me, into the shallow water, swam between my legs, and headed for the beach. My partner, who was following behind me, slammed his gaff into the salmon and dragged it ashore. That chinook weighted sixty-one pounds!

"You never know," he said, "what these salmon will do."

Many Kitimat salmon fishers are bottom-bouncers who cast heavy-gauge metal spoons out to midstream, where they let them drift down-river in the current, occasionally tap-tapping on the gravel river bottom. Spin-n-Glos and Birdy Drifters with sinkers are frequently used instead of spoons. Where the water is deep and the current is strong, still-fishing with artificial lures is extremely popular. The powerful current at the large pools along the lower river makes the use of four- to eight-ounce sinkers advisable. Spin-n-Glos in every conceivable color and size are the favorite lures of the still fisherman. Although Kitimat River anglers usually cast from shore, some fishing is done from drift boats. Cruising down the river in a small craft, boaters can easily get into holding water that is difficult to reach by car or on foot.

Citizens of Kitimat may tell you that Ron Wakita is the finest salmon fisherman who ever waded this river, and chances are they're absolutely right! Ron is a dedicated angler who loves his home river, knows its waters intimately, and is always ready and willing to assist visiting anglers in any way he can. One day I encountered Ron on the river, just after he lost a big chinook. He had chased it downstream as far as he could, and had waded out as deep as he dared. All in vain. The salmon continued on its downriver dash, leaving a helpless Ron Wakita far behind.

But Ron had a plan.

"Next time," he said, "I'm going to wear a wetsuit so I can just jump in and follow the fish down the river."

In the year 2000, Ron Wakita formed a company named "Reliable Guide and Charter Ltd." to operate on the Kitimat River and in the salty waters of Douglas Channel off the mouth of the great river. In Douglas Channel, the saltchuck anglers catch salmon and an endless variety of bottomfish, including tasty red snappers, lingcod and dozens of other denizens of the deep. The real muscle-straining fighters here are the big, battling halibut that commonly weigh between thirty and two hundred pounds. In 1998, Gary Schuett battled a 391-pound halibut for two hours and ten minutes in Douglas Channel before subduing it with the assistance of his wife Margaret and companions Godfrey Medhurst and Maxine Pass.

In addition to chinook salmon, the Kitimat River has steelhead, cutthroat trout, Dolly Varden char, chum salmon, pink salmon, sockeye salmon and coho salmon. Coho fishing in this fabulous stream

Ron Wakita with a clean, bright Kitimat River Chinook Salmon.
*Photo: Reliable Guide & Charter*

can be excellent, particularly in September. Although there are many anglers on the river at this time of year, it doesn't get as crowded as it does during the July chinook run. Cutthroat trout may be found in the Kitimat River at any time of the year. I have seen fat two-pound cutthroat feeding on salmon eggs in the river and its tributaries in late August, but the prime time for cutthroat (as well as Dolly Varden char) is from October to February, if heavy rains do not muddy the water.

Steelheading usually starts in March. Success can be spotty in the early season, but fishing often picks up in April. At the end of April and early in May, large numbers of steelhead enter the Kitimat, and many big, bright fish are taken at this time.

Although the Kitimat River and the throngs of chinook fishermen along its crowded banks in July is not my idea of a fun fishing situation, I must respect and admire a majestic waterway that produces seventy-pound salmon. How could we not love the stream that inspired fishing guide Noel Gyger to say, "This river, for its size, has more fish in it than any other river in the world"?

Halibut from Douglas Channel off the mouth of the Kitimat River.
*Photo: Ron Wakita*

## Gamefish Species

Chinook salmon, coho salmon, pink salmon, chum salmon, steelhead, cutthroat trout, Dolly Varden char.

## Regulations & Restrictions

- **Pink salmon:** non-retention.
- **Chinook salmon:** open April 1 to July 31 / 4 per day, but only one over 65 cm.
- **Coho salmon:** open April 1 to October 31 / 2 fish per day limit.
- **Chum salmon:** open April 1 to August 15 / 2 fish per day limit.
- **Steelhead:** 1 hatchery steelhead (hatchery fish have adipose fins removed) per day or 10 per month. Release all wild steelhead.
- **Cutthroat trout and Dolly Varden char:** 2 per day, but only one over 50 cm, and none under 30 cm. Barbless hook. Bait ban from May 15 to December 31. Check the latest fishing regulations before you begin to fish.

## Federal Fisheries

DFO <www.pac.dfo.mpo.gc.ca>

## Community Advisors

<pskf@direct.ca>

## Provincial Fish & Wildlife

<www.monday.com/fishing > For more information on fishing regulations, phone (250) 638-6530 and/or (877) 320-3467 and/or (250) 627-3436.

## Lures for Chinook Salmon & Coho Salmon

Gibbs Koho Spoons, Kitimat Spoon and Krocodile Spoons, in assorted sizes. Birdy Drifter, Spin-n-Glos, Pink Bubble Gum Plastic Worms and dozens of other spoons, spinners and plastic gee-gaws.

### Coho Flies

Cathy's Coat, Pearl Mickey Finn, Chartreuse Popsicle, Mylar Minnow, Coho Peacock, Coho Blue, Coho Sunset and Clouser Minnow. The Clouser Minnow was created by Bob Clouser to imitate shiners in Pennsylvania. Today, variations of the Clouser are used to catch most species of gamefish in North America. The important features of the Clouser are big dumbbell eyes and straight body materials.

### Steelhead Flies

Cowichan Special, Black Practitioner, Umpqua Special, Squamish Poacher, Skunk, McLeod Ugly, Davie Street Hooker, Woolly Worm, Cowichan Special.

### Natural Baits

Salmon eggs, dew worms (nightcrawlers), ghost shrimp. Bait is banned from May 15 to December 31.

## Guides, Outfitters, Charters, River Tours

### Reliable Guide & Charter Ltd.

380 City Center, Kitimat, BC, Canada V8C 1T6
Ron Wakita, proprietor. Phone (250) 632-3522
Reliable Guide & Charter has boats on the Kitimat River and in the saltwater of Douglas Channel where halibut weighing over 350 pounds have been boated.

### Northwest Fishing Guides

P.O. Box 434, Terrace, BC V8G 4B1
Noel Gyger, proprietor, Phone (250) 635-5295

# Tackle Shops

**City Center Home Hardware**
Fishing Tackle Department
380 City Center, Kitimat, BC, Canada V8C 1T6
Ron Wakita, Phone (250) 632-3522

**Cutty's Fly and Tackle**
325 City Center, Kitimat, BC, Canada
Phone (250) 632-5616

# Accommodations

**Radley Park Campground** on the North Kitimat River
56 sites (some with electric hookup), several riverside sites.
Phone (250) 632-7161

**Chalet Motel** in downtown Kitimat
820 Tsimshian Blvd., Kitimat, BC V8C 1T5.
Phone (250) 632-4615.

**City Center Motel**
480 City Center, Kitimat, BC V8C 1T5
Phone (250) 632-4848

# Highway Distances to the Kitimat River

**From**
- Vancouver, BC — 1396 km (867 miles)
- Blaine, WA (USA border crossing) — 1411 km (876 miles)
- Calgary, AB — 1429 km (887 miles)
- Edmonton, AB — 1379 km (856 miles)

# Kalum River

There is another fine river near the Kitimat, the great Kalum (alias Kitsumkalum) River. To get to the Kalum from the Kitimat, just drive north 58 kilometers on Highway 37 to Highway 16, then cross the bridge to Terrace. Head westward a few miles and you will reach a highway bridge over the lower reaches of the Kalum. This impressive and fish-rich waterway has good runs of steelhead that seem to be present in the Kalum almost all year 'round. Big chinook salmon (up to 85 pounds) begin to enter the river early in the summer, with July being the prime month. In August, some coho and pink salmon appear in the river. In September, anglers can expect to find summer steelhead, large coho (up to 25 pounds), as well as trout and Dolly Varden char.

### Guides for Kalum River
Noel Gyger's highly recommended company, Northwest Fishing Guides, is an obvious choice for Kalum River anglers. The Northwest company, with 16 years experience, has a fine sportfishing lodge located on Kalum Road, near the river. This non-smoking lodge has seven bedrooms, two lounge areas, patios, a great dining room and daily maid service.

Northwest Fishing Guides can escort anglers on 30 rivers and lakes in their neck of the woods.

Ask Noel Gyger about the salmon and Dolly Varden fishing in the Skeena River at the mouth of the Exchamsiks, Gitnadoix, Exstew and Zymagolitz rivers. He can also give you information on the Lakelse and Zymoetz rivers, as well as the salmon fishing in the big Skeena River. Phone Northwest Fishing Guides (250) 635-5295.

CHAPTER 2

# The Kispiox Kids

*In the Kispiox Valley, behind every tree, there is a Larson.*
— VIRGINIA LARSON

O n the next page, there is a delightful photograph of some very
young anglers—all residents of the Kispiox River Valley—who
have just returned from a successful trout-fishing expedition on their
home river, the Kispiox. This is a really great, unstaged picture of four
happy outdoors-loving country boys, each young lad with his own
individual expression and unique pose. In this photo, one thing is an
absolute certainly—all four boys are totally pleased with the results of
their fishing expedition. *They caught trout!* And as all of us old river-
worshippers know—catching fish is the name of the game!

This fine photo was submitted by Virginia Larson, the boss lady at
Sportsman's Kispiox Lodge, the only lodge and guiding service on
the river that caters to anglers all year round. The four lads—Sam
Larson, James de Boer, Conrad Larson and Ayden de Boer—are her
nephews. Fishing guides at Sportsman's Kispiox Lodge are Allan
Larson, Clint Larson, Gordon Wadley and Don Williams.

In the fall of 1954, a world record steelhead weighing thirty-six
pounds was taken from the Kispiox. The prestigious American
angling magazine *Field & Stream* published a feature story on the
almost-unknown remote Kispiox River, mentioning the startling fact
that, in 1954, six of the ten largest steelhead caught anywhere on earth
were hooked in the Kispiox. Not surprisingly, during the steelhead run
in 1955, and for many years hence, the banks of the Kispiox River
were crawling with anglers.

*Above:* The Kispiox Kids.
Left to right: Sam Larson,
James de Boer, Conrad Larson,
Ayden de Boer.

*Right:* Skeena River below
mouth of the Kispiox.

Today, in the new millennium, the famed Kispiox, with road access along its banks, continues to attract visiting anglers, including some from as far away as Japan, the southern United States and Europe. Thanks perhaps to some severe fishing regulations, including catch-and-release and barbless hook restrictions, the steelhead still migrate up the Kispiox River. September 1 to September 25 is a good bet for fishermen hoping to see the peak of the steelhead run.

The Kispiox River springs to life in the mountains of northern British Columbia, fifty-four kilometers east of Meziadin Lake and Meziadin Junction, then flows southeast through boreal forests of green fir and lodgepole pine—home of bears, moose, coyotes and bald eagles. It then empties into the mighty Skeena River at the historic aboriginal village of Kispiox, with its many old grey-weathered totem poles. This village was the home of the celebrated Robin Hood-style Indian outlaw Gunanoot, who eluded bounty hunters and police constables from 1906 to 1919 when he was charged with shooting two men. Gunanoot surrendered to the authorities after roaming the wilderness for thirteen years, somehow evading (with considerable assistance from sympathetic Kispiox residents) the police and the posses searching for him.

At his trial he was acquitted, possibly because of the Robin Hood reputation he acquired during his years as an outlaw.

Several miles south of Kispiox are three small villages: Old Hazelton, New Hazelton and South Hazelton, all clustered around the junction of the Bulkley and Skeena rivers. At Old Hazelton, tourists can visit 'Ksan, a historically authentic Indian village, with art studios, an exhibition center and the Northwestern National Museum.

Dwelling in the rugged wilderness of the upper Kispiox and Skeena rivers are Canada's most exotic mammals, the mystical white Kermode bears. In the past, many scientists believed these white bears were albinos, or polar bears that had strayed far from their arctic homeland. But it is now known that they are a sub-species of the common black bear. In the past the Indians believed the Kermodes were supernatural beings—white bears with the power to assume human form. According to ancient legend, the Kermodes change themselves into human beings to rescue people in distress, to fight evil forces, and to perform other good deeds.

The first time I gazed upon the tranquil waters of the Kispiox River, I was struck with its placid loveliness. During steelhead season,

*Above:* Tom Lee with 27-pound Kispian steelhead.
Photo: Virginia Larson

*Right:* Kispiox River steelhead.
Photo: Virginia Larson

the Kispiox Valley, with high mountains flanking the river, is a place of splendid natural beauty—in its lower reaches, the manicured emerald-green fields of the small streamside farms and the golden yellow poplar trees complement the blue water of the quiet stream. There are no waterfalls or large rapids on the Kispiox and wonder of wonders, boats with motors are banned!

But a word of warning! Because the Kispiox is fed by numerous small streams (and not by a lake) the creeks muddy up with even one day of heavy rain. This can result in the river becoming an opaque brown color, making fishing almost impossible.

## What's where ?
### And where is what ?

## Gamefish Species

■ Chinook salmon, coho salmon, pink salmon, chum salmon, steelhead, cutthroat, Dolly Varden, sockeye salmon.

■ Chinook (alias spring, king, quinnat) salmon enter the Kispiox in July. Open to angling June 16 to July 31 / 4 per day, only one over 65 cm. August 1 to August 31 / 4 per day, none over 65 cm.

■ Pink salmon open June 16 to Aug. 31 below boundary signs near the Kispiox River Resort. Limit is 2 per day.

■ Sockeye and chum salmon are completely catch-and-release.

■ Steelhead—the fish that made Kispiox famous. There are some steelhead in the river from late August to late October. Mid-September can be a good bet. Steelhead are totally catch-and-release.

■ There are resident trout in the Kispiox River, but many local anglers claim they usually are too small to be of much interest—possibly because these folks are used to very large salmon and steelhead. There are Dolly Varden char, too.

■ McQueen Creek (a tributary) is open year round for trout, and there is no bait ban on this stream. The creek is located almost directly across the Kispiox River from the Sportsman's Kispiox Lodge. 2 fish per day. No minimum size.

# Angling Methods

Fly fishing is extremely popular for the catch-and-release Kispiox steelhead, but spinning is popular too on this great waterway.

### Steelhead Flies

A few effective patterns are: Olive Woolly Bugger, Orange General Practitioner, Umpqua Special, Dynamite Stick, Polar Peril, Pynk Dynk, Summer Muddler, Lingren's Black Practitioner, Skinny Skunk and thousands of other well-known and unknown steelhead patterns.

### Steelhead Lures

Krocodile, Koho and Kitimat wobbling spoons, weighted spinners, fluorescent yarn and large Pink Bubble Gum plastic worms and Gooey Bobs.

### Lures for Chinook Salmon

Silver-colored wobbling spoons, Five of Diamonds spoons, Spin-n-Glos, Cherry Bobbers and weighted spinners.

### Flies for Pink Salmon

Pink Eve, Red Handlebar, Hoochie and a piece of red yarn knotted onto a bare hook.

# Gear Restrictions Etc.

Class 2 Classified Water: steelhead stamp mandatory Sept. 1 to Oct. 31. Single barbless hook all year round. Bait ban. Powerboats banned, and—wonder of wonders—no angling from boats.

For information on fishing regulations:
- phone BC Fish & Wildlife (250) 847-7303.
- Talking Yellow Pages (toll free) 1-877-320-3467.
- British Columbia Fisheries web site: www.bcfisheries.gov.bc.ca

# Guides, Charters, Outfitters, River Tours

**Sportsmans Kispiox Lodge**
Box 252, New Hazelton, BC, Canada V0J 2J0.
Phone (250) 842-6455.

This well-known lodge will arrange guided fishing trips for any time of the year. They keep at least four cabins open year round.

**Gordon Wadley, Kispiox River Tours**
Box 3429, Smithers, BC V0J 2N0

**Kispiox River Resort & Campground**
Housekeeping cabins.
Kispiox Valley Road, SM C46 RR1, Hazelton, BC V0J 1Y0.
Phone (250) 847-7320

Guided fishing: steelhead, salmon, trout, float trips.

**Hook and Line Guiding**
Wilfred Lee - Fishing Guide - Phone (250) 842-5337

# Fishing Tackle Shops

**Oscar's Source for Sports**
1214 Main Street, Smithers, BC, Canada V0J 2N0
Phone (250) 847-2136

**Misty River Tackle**
5008 Agar Avenue, Terrace, BC V8G 1J1
Phone (250) 638-1369

**Northcoast Anglers**
3217 Kalum Street, Terrace, BC V8G 2M8
Phone (250) 635-6499

# Accommodations

**Sportsmans Kispiox Lodge** on Kispiox Valley Road
Box 252, New Hazelton, BC, Canada V0J 2J0
Phone (250) 842-6455. Accommodations year round.

**Kispiox River Resort and Campground** on the Kispiox River
Kispiox Valley Road, SM C46 RR1, Hazelton, BC V0J 1Y0
Phone (250) 847-7320
Housekeeping cabins and tent sites

**Forest Service Recreation Sites**
On the Kispiox River there are three Forest Service Recreation Sites
that are suitable for overnight camping or day use. They are the
Lower Kispiox River, Sweetin River and upper Kispiox Ford
Recreation Sites. There is a minimal charge for camping in these
wilderness campgrounds. For information, phone Province of BC
Ministry of Forests (250) 842-6581 or (250) 638-8541. Visit the
Ministry of Forests website <http://for.gov.bc.ca>.

# Highway Distances to the Kispiox River

**From**
- Vancouver, BC — 1330 km (826 miles)
- Blaine, USA border crossing —1345 km (835 miles)
- Calgary, AB — 1363 km (846 miles)
- Edmonton, AB — 1312 km (815 miles)

While you are at the Kispiox River, ask the resort owners, campground operators or fishing guides for up-to-date information on the
fishing in the Bulkley and Morice Rivers. Both are along Highway
16, south of Kispiox/Hazelton, en route to Prince George.

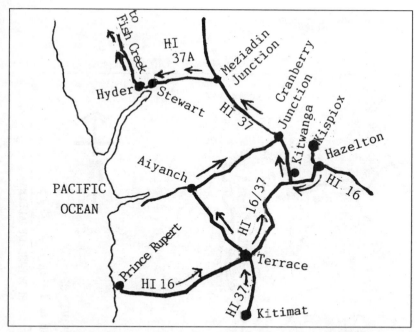

Roads from Kispiox to Stewart-Hyder and from Kitimat or Terrace to Stewart-Hyder.

## Bears and Eagles near the Kispiox River

Check out the unique wildlife area of Stewart-Hyder. Here's a great destination if you are an animal lover or a birdwatcher. From Kispiox/South Hazelton, drive southwest a few miles on Highway 16 to the aboriginal community of Kitwanga. At Kitwanga, take Highway 37 north to Meziadin Junction, then follow 37A west to Stewart, BC, and its nearby neighbor, Hyder, Alaska. It's a very short overall journey, actually. If you are starting from Kitimat, just head north on Highway 37 to Kitwanga.

At the village of Hyder you can see grizzly bears, black bears and white Kermode bears (alias "spirit bears"). The bears are here to feed on the salmon that spawn in Hyder's Fish Creek. July 7 to August 24 is the ideal time for bear-watching here.

The citizens of Hyder will tell you that the lower end of the Salmon River (near town) is the best place in the world for watching bald eagles feeding on salmon. Three species of Pacific salmon spawn here: the pink, coho and chum salmon. The local chum salmon have been known to reach a weight of 30 pounds—about twice the weight of a big chum in most watersheds.

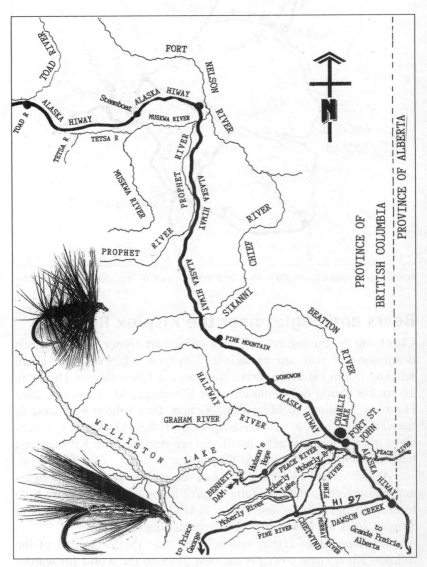

**Northern region of British Columbia — northeast section**

# CHAPTER 3

# The Toad Has Five Thousand Hats

plus the Kalum River

*The streams of the mountains please me more than the sea.*

— from the song "Guantanamera" by PETE SEEGER,
JOSE MARTI AND HECTOR ANGULO

An Alaska Highway stream, the Toad River is located in far northern British Columbia, approximately two hundred kilometers (130 miles) west of Fort Nelson. If you are heading for the Toad and you have to purchase any major items of fishing tackle, you'd better shop for them in the "big town" of Fort Nelson as you are driving through. This could save you a long drive back from the Toad River.

When approaching the community of Toad River, slow down at the Racing River Bridge. If you are an angler, you may wish to stop and check out this stream. The Racing River (at Mile 401) has produced sixteen-inch Arctic grayling and Dolly Varden char that weigh up to four pounds.

The small community of Toad River sits alongside the Alaska Highway near Mile 404. This tiny alpine settlement consists of several private homes, a school and a highway maintenance camp. It's not very big, but it is the largest community between Fort Nelson, BC and Watson Lake in the Yukon.

At Mile 405 you'll reach the Toad River Lodge with its world-famous collection of hats. Many years ago, some travelers left their caps hanging from the ceiling of the lodge's restaurant, and since then

The Toad River.

thousands of travelers have hung caps and hats and left them—now there are 5,250 colorful headpieces in the collection.

The lodge's restaurateurs serve terrific "home cooked" meals with bread, buns and other goodies fresh-baked daily. Toad River Lodge offers travelers a choice of accommodation—motel, cabins or level pull-through RV sites. Darryl Stevens and Matthew Roy, proprietors, will point out the spots where you'll find road access to the river.

You'll find the Poplars Campground at Mile 407, with its new cabins and forty large pull-through RV sites. Proprietors Dan and Vicky Clements are proud of their tasty cinnamon buns, foot-long hot dogs and fresh-fruit frozen yogurt. You will get your first glimpse of the turquoise waters of the Toad River at Mile 411. The northwest bound highway now follows the Toad for ten miles.

Throughout its length, the Toad River has a big, prolific population of Arctic grayling. As graceful as any fish that swims, the lovely grayling, with its large dorsal sailfin and its willingness to rise to a dry fly, is a first-rate game fish. During my brief but enjoyable sojourn on the banks of the splendid Toad River, every grayling I caught measured between twelve and sixteen inches. I know there must have been thousands of smaller fish in the river, but it was an uncommon treat not to hook any of them.

As birds soared overhead and a gentle breeze rustled the leaves of the trees at streamside, a big grayling made dimples on the glassy surface of a turquoise pool. For an old river worshiper like me, this was paradise. Standing knee-deep in the cold, clean water of the Toad River and drinking in the peace, serenity and beauty of the scenery, I couldn't help thinking that any angler who doesn't enjoy the delights of light-tackle grayling fishing doesn't have much of a sense of sportsmanship.

In the first twenty minutes of my first day on the Toad, below the mouth of a small creek, I nailed a fat sixteen-inch Arctic grayling and a fifteen-inch Dolly Varden, both on Dardevle wobbling spoons. After a couple of days I realized that something peculiar was happening. Here on the Toad, I was catching all my grayling on wobbling spoons that I was casting for Dollies. Spoons that are big enough to attract Dolly Varden char are, normally, of no interest to grayling. Before I visited the Toad River, I had almost always caught grayling on tiny dry flies.

Pauline, who is an expert seafood chef, barbecued the smaller twelve- and thirteen-inchers. We have found that, before cleaning grayling, it's best to grab them by the tails and scrape off all the scales. Then simply gut them, behead them, butter them, and barbecue them whole.

When I fished the Toad in 1992, I enjoyed fair success with Dolly Varden, considering my fishing forays were of short duration— always less than three hours—and usually I was within sight of the Alaska Highway. Late one afternoon, near the highway bridge, I caught a prime nineteen-inch Dolly Varden on a half-ounce chrome Krocodile wobbler. The next fish to hit the Krocodile was a twelve-inch Arctic grayling. I was shocked to see a small-mouthed fish like a grayling attacking that big, flashy piece of metal. Fishing along this same stretch was river angler Wally Seymour of Vernon, British Columbia. He landed a five-pound Dolly, and lost another one that would have topped three pounds. Nearby, while Wally was battling his two fish, I watched an American tourist beaching two fifteen-inch Dollies. All this action—right along the shoulder of the highway!

On the Toad River, and on virtually all other northern British Columbia streams, the Dolly Varden char (alias bull trout) is a sport

Gordon Davies holding a small Dolly Varden and a good-sized Arctic Grayling.

fish of major importance—and why not? These thick-bodied, silvery, north country Dollies are eager biters and creditable fighters; they also taste great when cleaned, filled with bread stuffing and baked in the oven. And, if you are a gourmet chef, try poaching the Dolly Varden in white wine. Incidentally, some locals claim the Toad's Dollies can weigh over six or seven pounds.

Before I leave the subject of Dolly Varden fishing, I must relate the following tale. I know I shouldn't mention this at all, but I just can't help myself.

An angler who lives in the Great White North told me—before the present bait ban was implemented—that this was how he fished for Dolly Varden—and he caught huge Dollies all his life. First, he captured a supply of mice in a live trap, then he took the live mice with him to the river. Positioning himself at the head of a good pool, he knotted a large hook to his line, tied the hook to the mouse's back and placed the critter on a flat piece of wood. He launched the flat board and let the whole assembly drift into the middle of the pool. Then he pulled the mouse off the board. The guy claimed that, invariably, the swimming mouse was grabbed by a gigantic Dolly Varden.

Rather gruesome but, admittedly, quite innovative.

If you'd like to benefit from the help of professional outdoorsmen in the Toad River area, give one of these fellows a call—Dale Drinkall of Folding Mountain Outfitters or Dave Wiens of Stone Mountain Safaris. Both men are listed in the "What's Where" section at the end of this chapter. You will find a list of campgrounds and lodges in the same section.

We residents of Canada's far-west province sometimes forget how fortunate we are in having an enormous variety of wildlife. British Columbia has twenty-five per cent of the world's grizzly bear population, twenty-five per cent of the bald eagles, half of the earth's blue grouse, half of the trumpeter swans, sixty per cent of the mountain goats and seventy-five per cent of all the stone sheep on the planet. The rugged, mountainous country around the Toad River is the home of several bands of stone sheep. These agile mountain dwellers are regularly observed along the shoulder of the Alaska Highway, where they gather to lick the salts and minerals in the roadside gravel.

There are plenty of bears in this northern valley, both blacks and grizzlies. Larger than black bears, the grizzlies are the unchallenged monarchs of the boreal forest. Their coats vary in color from brown

Summertime fishing on Northern B.C.'s Toad River.

to cream to black, with long, white or silver guard hairs, giving the big bears a grizzled appearance, hence the name "grizzly". They attain weights of over half a ton but, in spite of their large size, the powerful animals can run at speeds up to thirty miles an hour. In flight, grizzly bears run straight ahead through the bush—unlike most other animals that zig and zag around trees until they reach the safety of the deep woods. These big brutes can charge straight uphill with the power of Sherman tanks.

The Toad River is located about as far north as it possibly could be within the boundaries of the province of British Columbia. Rising high in the Suskwa Range of the Rocky Mountains, the wild Toad rambles northward, through Moose Lake, then joins the West Toad River and gathers in the flow of Tandzie Creek, several miles west of the tiny hamlet of Toad River. The stream now runs in an easterly direction, its waters reflecting the slim, dark green trees of the spruce forest. Flowing alongside the craggy mountains and past the Toad River settlement, the stream wanders northeast to empty its sparkling blue-green waters into the big Liard River at the Yukon border.

For any river fisher contemplating a far-northern summertime fishing trip, the Toad offers some good light tackle fun, particularly if the visiting angler brings a shallow-draft boat for exploring pools and runs that are beyond highway access. A sport fisherman may find more than good fishing on this alpine stream. A few relaxing days on the glorious Toad can leave the angler feeling spiritually and physically renewed.

Midsummer is a good time for a Toad River vacation. Warm weather is more or less assured, but no season of the year here is free from frequent sudden changes in weather. Windstorms and rainstorms come and go without warning. Mosquitoes and black flies are sure to be bothersome, so take a supply of insect repellents and after-bite treatments.

# What's where ?
## And where is what ?

## Gamefish Species
- Dolly Varden char (alias bull trout) to five pounds or more in remote stretches.
- Arctic grayling, up two or three pounds.

## Regulations & Restrictions
- Closed to fishing April 1 to June 30.
- Single hook. Bait ban.

## Daily Catch Limit
- Dolly Varden (bull trout) one per day, 30 to 50 cm, Oct. 16 to Aug. 14. Catch-and-release Dolly Varden Aug. 15 to Oct. 15.
- Arctic grayling: two per day (none under 30 cm in length, and only one over 45 cm may be kept).

## Possession Limits
- For grayling or Dolly Varden (bull trout): possession limit equals one daily catch limit.

## Angling Methods
Usually fly fishing and spinning.

**Lures for Dollies**
Krocodile, Dardevle, Five-of-Diamonds, Koho spoons.

**Flies For Arctic Grayling**
- Dry Flies: No. 14-20: Black Wulff (a moose hair floater), Irresistible, Humpy and Tom Thumb (deadly deer hair floaters), Mosquito, Black Bivisible, Brown Bivisible.
- Wet Flies: No. 10-16: Black Ant, Grey Shrimp, Black Woolly Worm, Black Gnat, Cowdung.

## Outfitters, River Tours, Guides, Charters

**Dave Wiens, Stone Mountain Safaris**
Box 7870, Toad River, BC V0C 2X0
Phone (250) 232-5469.

**Dale Drinkall, Folding Mountain Outfitters Ltd**
Box 27, Mile 422, Alaska Highway, Toad River, BC V0C 2X0
Phone (250) 232-5451

# Tackle Shops

It is unlikely you'll find a really extensive variety of fishing tackle in the Toad River area. It's best to do your shopping in Fort Nelson before heading further along the Alaska Highway to the river. Here is one recommended store in Fort Nelson:

**C.M.P. Sports**
Lou Carew, proprietor
Box 1048, Fort Nelson, BC, Canada V0C 1R0
Phone (250) 774-2944

# Accommodations

**Toad River Lodge**
Darrel Stevens and Matthew Roy, proprietors
Mile 405, Alaska Highway, BC, Canada V0C 2X0
Phone (250) 232-5401, Fax (250) 232-5215

Motel, cabins, pull-through RV sites with full hook-ups. Stand-up barbecue pits, free firewood, laundromat, hot showers. Service station-gas, diesel, propane, tire repairs, 24-hour towing, airstrip, restaurant.

**Poplars Campground and Café**
Dan and Vicky Clements
Box 30, Toad River, BC, Canada V0C 2X0
Phone (250) 232-5465

Mile 407, Alaska Highway, 4 miles northbound past Toad River Community. Level, treed, pull-through campsites. Cabins for travelers. Gas and diesel.

**Stone Mountain Safaris Lodge** (Open May 1 to Oct. 30)
Box 7870, Toad River, BC, Canada V0C 2X0
Phone (250) 232-5469

Lot 2031, Mile 428 Alaska Highway. Turn right off Alaska Highway, 9 kilometers north of village of Toad River. A ranch-style lodge, with horseback riding, adventure tours, hiking.

# Highway Distances to The Toad River

**From:**

- Vancouver, BC — 1761 km (1093 miles)
- Blaine, WA, USA — border crossing - 1778 km (1099 miles)
- Calgary, AB — 1524 km (946 miles)
- Edmonton, AB — 1231 km (764 miles)

---

**For more information on Toad River**,
contact the Northern B.C. Tourism Association.

Phone 1-800-663-8843 / Fax (250) 847-5227
Email: info@northernbctourisn.bc.ca

**For updated information on fishing regulations:**

Phone (250) 774-3547
B.C. Fisheries web site <www.bcfisheries.gov.bc.ca>

# CHAPTER 4

# Moberly Dick's River
plus Halfway River

*Never kill a fish in the presence of a purist. Simply play your fish behind a big tree before bashing its head in. Then stuff it in your chest waders.*

— GERRY MCNALLY

Residing in the depths of Moberly Lake, near the town of Chetwynd in northern British Columbia, is a gigantic, fire-breathing reptilian monster named Moberly Dick. Older than time, Dick is the guardian of the lake and protector of all people, mammals, reptiles and birds living in the Moberly Valley.

On the shore of the lake at the West Moberly Indian Reserve, a middle-aged lady told me she first heard of the monster from a tribal elder when she was a young girl. "At the bottom of Moberly Lake," she explained, "there are mountains, hills, valleys and canyons. And below the lake bottom and its valleys and mountains there is another lake. This lake-under-the-lake is the home of the monster."

I asked the woman about the name 'Moberly Dick.' "The lake monster doesn't have a name," she replied, "We just call it 'the monster.'"

Because I learned of the name 'Moberly Dick' in a newspaper story, it is safe to assume that it was the brainchild of a newspaper scribe or a Chamber of Commerce publicist.

The clean, clear, icy waters of the wild upper Moberly River tumble down the uninhabited mountain slopes northeast of the communi-

The Moberly River is the home of Dolly Varden char and Arctic grayling while Moberly Lake has good populations of lake trout and pike.

ty of Mackenzie. The river winds its way through fastwater rapids and slow, deep pools, much of the time surrounded by an almost inaccessible forest, before it enters the west end of Moberly Lake. Leaving the east end of the lake, the river moves in a northeasterly direction, often flowing quite swiftly, through a sparsely-populated countryside, before it joins the mighty Peace River a few miles southwest of the city of Fort St. John.

There is fairly easy road access into much of the stream above Moberly Lake, where anglers can find Arctic grayling, Dolly Varden and mountain whitefish. Because of its narrow or shallow stretches, the Moberly River is unsuitable for most boats. Almost all fishing guides in this neck of the woods use boats on the rivers, so it is virtually impossible to find a guide who will work on the Moberly. But if anglers need directions, they'll find the folks in nearby tackle shops extremely helpful. One local outfitter, Armand Didier, has offered to answer queries from visitors or potential visitors. Phone or fax him at (250) 788-2860.

Throughout its length the Moberly River is the home of Dolly Varden char and Arctic grayling. Pike are sometimes found around the mouth of the river and in the Peace River near the Moberly's mouth. To get to the confluence of the Moberly and Peace rivers from the town of Chetwynd, drive north and take the Jackpine turn-off. Follow it until the road runs alongside the Moberly River. You will now be in an area known as Del Rio, bordered by the Moberly River, the lower Pine River, and the Peace River.

In July 1995, Pauline and I were fishing the upper Moberly River

Veteran Moberly River angler, Brian Baker, on the wild and lovely Moberly.

with Brian Baker and his wife Sherry. Brian and Sherry are as knowledgeable about the Moberly River and its fish as anyone you are ever likely to meet. At one large, deep pool, Sherry took a nice Arctic grayling on a weighted spinner. I landed a plump fourteen-inch grayling that grabbed my Tom Thumb fly, and Pauline—who said she was tired of casting—took her camera and trotted off in pursuit of a large doe deer that had been hanging around our camper, as curious about us as we were about her.

Brian, meanwhile, was encountering one problem after another. He wasn't fishing for grayling. Brian was after Dollies. A master Dolly Varden angler, he knows exactly where the Dollies rest in every accessible pool on the Moberly. Wearing his Polaroid glasses, he does a visual check of all the good holding water. If he spots a Dolly Varden, he puts a wiggly plastic worm-like lure on his hook, casts his still-fishing rig into the water in front of the fish's nose, then sits down and waits. On this occasion Brian was using a small, bright yellow, fork-tailed, soft plastic wiggling worm. This type of lure had always been a real killer for him, but on this day everything was going wrong.

He spotted a Dolly in one of his regular hot spots, then cast his surefire yellow plastic worm into the hole and waited. Brian got a couple of bites, then nothing. When he reeled in, he saw that a fish had bitten the tail end off his forky-tailed worm, so he removed the severed lure, impaled a new one on his hook, cast into the pool, and again waited for action. At this juncture, an elderly Labrador retriever appeared on the bank across the river from him, plunged into the water, swam across, clambered up out of the river and sat down beside Brian and shivered. Brian moved the wet pooch into a sunny spot to warm up, and then went back to fishing. Once more he got a couple of bites, then the action ceased. Checking his lure, he again found it bitten in half. Brian didn't fare much better with his next yellow wiggle-worm. He hooked a respectable-sized fish, fought it for a considerable time and then began to lead it toward the marge of the river. But suddenly, inexplicably, his line went slack, his hook pulled out and there on the hook, snagged through the tail, was a small partially digested whitefish. What a revolting development! Unlikely as it seems, a Dolly Varden must have swallowed the fork-tailed strip of plastic, and the hook became embedded in the rear end of a small fish the Dolly was digesting. At the same spot, Brian got another bite, then nothing more. He checked the plastic worm and, sure enough, the tail

Gordon Davies fly-fishing for arctic grayling on the Moberly River.

was chopped off. As if that wasn't enough, it happened once more—another lure cut cleanly in half. Brian was more than somewhat unhappy, but he wasn't about to give up. With a glance at the old Lab, who was now snoozing happily in the warm rays of the sun, Brian tied on another plastic wiggler and chucked it into the same place in the same pool. A good bite and the yellow wiggler was chopped in half again. On his next cast, things began to look brighter. A fish hit hard, Brian set the hook solidly, then began to play a good Dolly. The fish was tiring and the veteran river angler was leading it into shore, but fate intervened. Before it got into shallow water, the Dolly swam around a submerged tree branch. The best thing to do in this situation is to throw out some slack line, then sit down and hope the fish will swim back in the opposite direction and free the line. This is exactly what Brian started to do, but right at that moment his sleeping canine buddy awoke, jumped into the water and swam across the fishing line, breaking it and allowing the fish to escape. Things really couldn't get worse, and fortunately they didn't. On his next cast he hooked and landed a sixteen-inch Dolly Varden and took it home for supper. When he gutted the fish, he could hardly believe what he found in its stomach: four yellow plastic fork-tails!

The Moberly is an ideal stream for anglers—big enough to support large populations of fish, but not too wide for the wading fisherman to cover with comparative ease. Like many other northern rivers, it has some accessible pools and runs, but it has many more that are totally or almost totally, inaccessible. And, like a majority of northern streams, the Moberly has Dolly Varden char, large numbers of prolific mountain whitefish, and a fairly good population of Arctic grayling—the freshwater fly caster's dream fish.

It has been my extreme good fortune over the past fifteen years to have made several safaris into the grayling rivers of northern British Columbia, the Yukon and northern Alberta. One trip lasted four months, from June to September. The result of these forays is that I have become totally addicted to fly fishing for Arctic grayling. The lovely grayling, with its high gray-mauve-black sailfin, is often found at the head of a deep pool or run, immediately below fast water. In my personal opinion, dry flies (number twelve to twenty) brown, black or gray in color are most productive. Having said that, I must confess I've also taken grayling on number eight bright yellow bee imitations, number six Woolly Worms, small weighted spinners, small spoons and even a one-ounce chrome Krocodile wobbler.

However, nothing will take grayling better than small dry flies, particularly deer hair patterns like the Tom Thumb, Irresistible and Humpy. The deer hair flies float well, even in whitewater rapids, which is a tremendous advantage for a mediocre fly-caster like me.

On a summer afternoon, Pauline and I set up camp off the road, near a couple of likely-looking pools. While reconnoitering, I spotted an angler fishing from atop a large boulder several hundred yards upstream. As I was watching him, he gathered up his gear and started hiking down the river toward me. I waited, and when he arrived I saw that he had caught a three-pound Dolly Varden. I had my fly rod with me, so I hiked up to the rock he had vacated (it overlooked a big fishy-looking pool) to see if I could find a pair of grayling for supper. Standing on the steeply-sloping boulder, I watched several grayling feeding on the surface. I tossed my dry fly upstream into the white water at the head of the pool and watched it float through the deeper, slower water. I had rises from some ten- to fourteen-inch grayling, but they just rolled near the fly without attempting to inhale it. Eventually one fish smashed the fly with considerable force. I set the hook, played the grayling, then—having no landing net—I pulled him up, hand over hand, to the top of the rock. A good twelve-incher. One for the pot, and now I needed one more so we could have a fish apiece for supper.

It was late afternoon before I hooked another grayling, and I was anxious to get back to camp with some fish before Pauline started to cook macaroni or wieners for supper. But when I worked this one in close to the big boulder, I saw that the fly was hooked insecurely in the skin at the outer edge of its lip. I knew I couldn't successfully haul this one up out of the water to the top of the rock. Without a net, I had to improvise. I had a pair of very long, slender, needle-nose pliers in my pocket, and I reasoned that I could grab the graying by the jaw with the pliers, then easily lift it to my perch atop the boulder. I slid down the rock as far as I dared; then, holding the rod in my left hand to keep the fish's head at the surface, I reached down with the pincers in my right hand, grabbed what was supposed to be the grayling's jaw, and lifted. Then I saw my fish swimming away, safe and sound. And I noticed, that all I had grabbed with the pliers was the fly. I never did catch a second grayling for supper that afternoon, but I did land a foot-long whitefish, which Pauline barbecued along with the grayling.

The green-forested Moberly Valley in summertime is adorned with brightly colored wildflowers, including goldenrod, monkshood, cow parsnip, fireweed, meadowrue, Arctic lupine and fringed aster with its pale blue flowers. In this northern paradise you'll find Saskatoon berries, tasty wild raspberries, gooseberries, thimbleberries and wild strawberries. Moberly evergreen trees include the tall and straight lodgepole pine, subalpine fir, black spruce, white spruce, Engelmann spruce, and the short, shrubby Rocky Mountain juniper. There is also a trailing evergreen shrub, the kinnikinnick, which the Indian people once blended with their pipe tobacco. Some local deciduous trees are alder, birch, aspen, poplar, dogwood, choke cherry and pin cherry.

When we weren't camping and fishing along the river we lived in our camper van on the lakeshore. During our daytime fishing and photographing trips, we left some of our gear in the lakeside campground, piled on and around a picnic table in our campsite. One item we always left behind was an icebox that contained a few dozen worms. Since we weren't using natural bait on the Moberly River, the worms were just excess baggage. Returning to our lakeside campsite from the river one day we noticed that the worm box was missing. Seven or eight young kids were playing on a lawn nearby. I walked over and asked them, "Did anybody see an ice box at our campsite?" The entire gang pointed at one little six-year-old boy and, in unison, announced, "He stole it!" The poor kid sprinted away and disappeared amongst a group of parked trailers. "Well," I thought, "that's the last I'll see of my icebox or the little boy." But I was wrong on both points, because the young fellow returned carrying the icebox. With a whipped-pup look on his face, he handed me the box. I looked inside and it was empty. "Where are the worms?" I asked. His reply was a classic. He looked me straight in the eye and said "I set them free." I wasn't annoyed with that cute little kid, but I couldn't help remembering I had paid a teenage lad six dollars to dig those worms—and I hadn't used any of them!

Summertime visitors to the Moberly Valley are invited to join in the festivities at the annual Pemmican Days celebration on the Salteau Band Reserve at the east end of Moberly Lake. A few unusual events are a moose-calling competition, a tea-boiling contest, axe-throwing competition, pancake-eating contest and an open-fire bannock-making competition.

In midsummer the West Moberly Reserve at the other end of the lake holds its annual West Moberly Days celebrations, with a volleyball tournament, leg wrestling competition, bow and arrow shooting, a horseshoe tournament, cow-calling contest, moccasin races and bingo all day long.

Moberly Lake offers good fishing for lake trout if you have a boat. Twelve- to sixteen-pounders are caught here. Lack of a boat isn't really a handicap because Moberly Lake Marina will rent you one of its excellent rental boats. The lake has a population of pike (alias jacks, snakes, jackfish) as well as the lake trout.

When you are fishing on the lake, be sure you keep your camera ready. You may get some good photos of Moberly Dick.

# What's where ?
## And where is what ?

## Gamefish Species
Arctic grayling, mountain whitefish, Dolly Varden Char.

In long narrow Moberly Lake—this lake separates the upper river from the lower river, like a widening of the river—there are big lake trout (many well over 10 pounds) and large pike (alias jackfish).

## Seasons
From July 1 (after high water drops) until late September if weather is mild. (Bring insect repellent in summer.)

## Closure
The river is closed to fishing from April 1 to June 30.

# Restrictions
- Single hook, bait ban.

For detailed info on possible changes in (or info on) regulations:
- B.C. Fisheries website www.bcfisheries.gov.bc.ca
- B.C. Fish & Wildlife phone (250) 788-3611

# Angling Methods
- Fly fishing and ultralight spinning for grayling.
- Spinning and wet fly fishing for Dollies.

# Lures & Flies

### For Grayling & Whitefish
- Dry Flies: smallish Humpy, Tom Thumb, Bivisible, and almost any somber-hued number 10 to 20 dry or wet patterns.
- Smallest sizes weighted spinners.

### For Dolly Varden
- Medium-size silver, red or fluorescent orange wobbling spoons.
- Also lead head jigs with fluorescent pink, orange or red wiggle-type plastic bodies.

# Guides, Outfitters, Tackle Shops
It appears that fishing guides don't like to work on the Moberly River because the stream has many narrow or shallow stretches that are impossible to navigate in drift boats. However, two reliable local fishing tackle dealers have offered to help visiting anglers in any way possible:

### Back Country Sports
10040 100 Street, Fort St. John, BC, Canada V1J 3Y4
Phone (250) 785-1461.

**Lone Star Sporting Goods**
5028 50th Ave., Chetwynd, BC V0C 1J0
Phone (250) 788-1850
Contact: Carl Rhodes

**Armand Didier**
PO Box 1057, Chetwynd, BC, Canada V0C 1J0
Phone (250) 788-2860.

Outfitter Armand Didier says he will be happy to answer queries from anglers about the Moberly. If you contact Armand about the Moberly, also ask him about the float trips he is planning for the nearby wild Murray, lovely Pine, Wolverine and Sukunka rivers.

**Moberly Lake Marina**
Phone (250) 788-2050 (summer season)
Contact: Tim Thompson

Tim Thompson and his gang at Moberly Lake Marina have offered to help with tips and directions for the upper Moberly River and, of course, they can give you first-hand information on fishing for large lake trout in Moberly Lake. (There are good-sized pike also in the lake.) They have some fine, fast boats for rent at their marina.

A big, big dolly! Kim McLeod of Fort St. John with a 25-pound Dolly Varden from the Lower Halfway River.

# Accommodations

**Moberly Lake Provincial Park Campground**
on south side of Moberly Lake, three kilometers off Highway 29.
109 sites. Phone (250) 787-3407. (seasonal)

**Caron Creek RV Park**
PO Box 551, Chetwynd, BC V0C 1J0.
Full service pull-through sites. 30 amp power. Grass sites, 15 amp
power. Phone Allen or Lorrie (250) 788-2522.

**Westwind RV Park**
50 pull-through sites. Full hookups. Playground. Phone David or
Laurie Gayse (250) 788-2190. Box 2157, Chetwynd, BC V0C 1J0

**Lynx Creek RV Park and Campground**
Box 149, Hudson's Hope, BC V0C 1V0. Phone Kip or Julie
Howard (250) 783-5333.

**Moberly Lake Resort Marina**
Cabins and boats for rent. Phone (250) 788-2050.

# Highway Distances to Moberly River

**From:**

- Vancouver, BC — 1160 km (720 miles)
- Blaine, WA, USA border crossing — 1150 km (714 miles)
- Calgary, AB — 980 km (608 miles)
- Edmonton, AB — 690 km (428 miles)

# Halfway River

There is a big, wild river near the Moberly—the Halfway River.

An angler can drive into a part of the Halfway River from the south end of the Alaska Highway, but to find the most productive water in this wild and sparsely populated country, visitors should hire an experienced, local, professional guide.

The attraction here is the abundance of fifteen-to-twenty-pound-plus Dolly Varden char.

Fishing guide Rick Hopkins of Custom River Adventures can take you into the best spots on the Halfway and its fishy tributary, the Graham River. For more details phone Rick at (250) 785-1672. Email: hopkins@pris.bc.ca

Mailing address: Custom River Adventures, RR 1, S8, C32, Fort St. John, BC, Canada V1J 4M6.

# CHAPTER 5

# Cliff Andrews' Tetsa River
plus the Sikanni Chief River

*Pound for pound, the Arctic grayling can fight as well as any rainbow trout.*

— OLLIE TJADER

The Tetsa River Valley is the home of ravens, jays, kestrels and regal bald eagles. Cunning owls hunt rodents in the lupine, clover and fireweed-carpeted meadows; nighthawks dive-bomb mosquitoes at dusk. Falcons soar on thermals at high elevations; goshawks race between the poplars, pines and skinny spruce trees in pursuit of unsuspecting squirrels and chipmunks. In the surrounding boreal forests are caribou, deer, record-size elk and moose. There are grizzlies—lots of them—and big black bears. And there are people with Bear Scare Stories. Some of these stories are mildly entertaining, some are rather exciting, but a few are downright terrifying! Cliff Andrews, the head wrangler at Tetsa River Outfitters, has a remarkable Bear Scare Story. Here is his tale of terror:

"Tenting in the bush in the early 1980s, I was enjoying a peaceful night's sleep when suddenly I was awakened by a grating, rumbling sound. I had no idea what time it was, but I knew I hadn't been asleep for very long. The rumbling sound was a slight annoyance. Snow had been falling steadily throughout the evening, so I figured the noise was just an accumulation of the white stuff sliding off the fly of the tent. Was I wrong! The rumbling continued, and the beam of my flashlight revealed the head and shoulders of the largest black bear I had ever seen! The big bear was pressing forward through a gaping gash it had torn in the tent. The rumbling, grating sound turned out to be a guttural growl emanating from the heavy chest and throat of the huge animal.

"With thought processes that took about one second, I realized I had plenty of ammunition within easy reach but, unfortunately, my rifle was six feet away at the opposite side of the tent. I did the only thing I could do. I let out a blood-curdling yell and, believe me, it was a realistic imitation of a frightened hunter. Luckily, the bear backed off. It worked! Temporarily, that is. But before I had time to breathe a sigh of relief, I heard the big bruiser shuffling along the outside of the tent, right beside my sleeping bag. The tent shook, then a massive paw ripped through the canvas right above me. The long claws didn't miss me by more than a few inches.

"Again I hollered, and the paw disappeared. But a couple of seconds later the powerful critter tore another hole at the far corner of the

Tetsa River Arctic Grayling.

tent. Ropes, pegs and poles flew everywhere, and the shredded corner of the tent collapsed. At this point I let loose with a third piercing scream of terror. Evidently, this was too much for the big beast, which scampered off into the deep woods. For the rest of the night, I admit, I was too wide-awake to get back to sleep."

The Tetsa is one of the finest small accessible grayling streams in northern British Columbia. Located a short distance from the town of Fort Nelson on the Alaska Highway, and south of the Yukon and Northwest Territories, the Tetsa is right smack in the middle of some of Canada's best Arctic grayling country.

In the wild hills southwest of Fort Nelson, the main fork of the Tetsa River flows from four small mountain lakes, drops over a lovely waterfall and rambles north through spruce and pine forest to the Alaska Highway. The tiny North Tetsa rises near Summit Lake in the highest mountain pass on the entire Alaska Highway. It joins the main Tetsa River near Mile 379 on the highway. There is easy access to the stream between Mileposts 365 and 378 on the great highway. West of Mile 364, and all the way to its confluence with the big Muskwa River, the Tetsa is virtually inaccessible by auto, truck or RV. Ask Cliff Andrews at Tetsa River Outfitters and Campground about taking you into remote areas.

Arctic grayling, as their name suggests, live in the cold rivers and lakes of the northland, mainly in the Arctic drainage. They are gray, brown or silvery on the back and sides, with v- or x-shaped black spots on the fore-part of the body. When light strikes at certain angles, a freshly caught fish sometimes has a brassy, lilac-colored sheen. The pectoral fins, anal fins and tail usually are dusky chartreuse, but the pelvic fins commonly have obscure stripes of black and pink. Because its diet consists mainly of insects, the grayling is the ideal quarry for the fly caster.

On the table, the meat of the Arctic grayling ranks with the best. The flesh is firm and moist and has a delicate flavor without a trace of the normal 'fishy' taste common to most species. Grayling meat should never be frozen because the freezing process can soften the flesh and spoil the flavor. I really enjoy eating grayling. On a four-month fishing safari along the rivers of northern British Columbia and the Yukon Territory, I discovered that I could eat barbecued grayling for dinner almost every day and never tire of it. This fact alone is enough to lure me back to the north country.

But fishing and eating aren't the only things that tempt me to return to the wild valley of the Tetsa. I can hear the siren call of the river's melodious singing waters, and I remember the evergreen-treed mountains with their resident grizzlies and black bears. I envision the fields covered with masses of purple, yellow, white and flame-colored summer wildflowers, and I long for the peace and serenity of the wilderness. An old river worshiper such as I could not possibly resist the call of the wild Tetsa River.

There are some big grayling in the Tetsa River, and the largest specimens tend to be quite chunky and heavy in the belly. A sixteen- to seventeen-incher will weigh about two pounds. A fat twenty-inch Tetsa grayling that tipped the scales at three pounds was taken from this stream near Tetsa River Lodge a few years ago by angler Reg Franzen. You can see a newspaper clipping with a story and a photo of Reg's fat grayling at Tetsa River Lodge.

Ollie Tjader, a former resident of the Alaska Highway town of Fort Nelson, BC, has caught his fair share of grayling from the waters of the Tetsa. He is a fly fisher par excellence as well as an accomplished fly tyer, and he knows this pretty waterway as intimately as anyone who ever fished here. In his younger years, Ollie lived in Kamloops where he learned the honorable crafts of fly tying and fly casting for rainbow trout from an old master, the late Jack Shaw, who was undoubtedly the greatest fly fisherman in the Kamloops area.

Ollie points out that the grayling is a great fighter. It certainly is! And, in addition to its fighting ability, the Arctic grayling has another important attribute—it is the most beautiful freshwater game fish in Canada. Its high, black-spotted, sail-like dorsal fin—edged in pale pink or white—distinguishes this graceful fish from all other species.

Tom Thumb, an excellent fly for Arctic Grayling.

Tetsa River near Tetsa Outfitters.

Some anglers will tell you that an Arctic grayling seldom jumps. But I have seen many of the Tetsa's fourteen- to sixteen-inchers, when hooked, leap straight up in the air. In the summer of 1992, when I was fly fishing for Arctic grayling near Tetsa River Outfitters' Lodge, I found a particularly attractive stretch of water. Where some medium-fast shallows flowed into a fine pool, there were fish feeding in the shallow water and in the pool. Knee-deep wading put me within easy casting distance of all the productive water.

I spotted two fairly large grayling feeding on the surface. I cast to the nearer fish but it showed no interest in my number fourteen dry Mosquito fly, so I offered it to the other feeding grayling and he socked it. As I played the fish I could feel its weight, and I was certain it was a two- or three-pounder. When the grayling weakened and I had him coming toward me, I selected a spot on the gravel shore where I could easily slide the fish out of the river. Then it jumped and the hook pulled out. That fish was big! And fat!

Although I continued to fish this pool for another hour, I didn't hook any more exceptional grayling. I nailed some smaller ones on dry flies and I caught a couple of mountain whitefish on a number ten wet Black Gnat.

Next morning I returned to the same pool, made a few casts with a number twelve Tom Thumb, and was shocked to find myself tied to another heavy, hard-fighting grayling. I played this fish right off the reel, and I was careful not to apply any drag other than the slight tension afforded by the click on the fly reel. When it appeared to be tiring and was fifteen feet from shore, it sailed skyward. Suspended in space for a millisecond was a large, lovely, chubby Arctic grayling. But when the fish dropped back into the water, my line was limp. I couldn't believe it. I really was sure I had just lost the same fish two days in a row! To make matters worse, I hooked three more fish—not large ones—and lost all of them. I guess I must be a glutton for punishment because I hiked right back to my "Bad Luck Pool" the following day. I was not feeling over-confident. Soon after I began casting I hooked a fish—again not a large one—and, although I played it with great care, the hook and the fish parted company.

"Well," I said to myself, "here I go again. Looks like I will never land another fish". I spotted another grayling rising across and downstream. When I floated a Tom Thumb over the fish, it took the fly while performing the graceful semi-roll that is the trademark of surface-feeding Arctic grayling. I set the hook, then played the fish with excessive caution, because I desperately wanted to bag this one. I knew it was large and I was expecting it to jump, as all the big Tetsa grayling seemed wont to do. And, sure enough, when it was less than twenty feet away from me it shot into the air, dropped back into the water and immediately jumped again. My heart skipped a few beats. I hadn't lost it! Moments later I slid the grayling onto the gravel bar. It was fat and heavy and measured sixteen inches. And then I received an unexpected, but not unpleasant, shock. After handling the fish very gently—playing it with extreme care—I discovered that there had been absolutely no need at all for the kid glove treatment. The fly could never have pulled loose because it was firmly embedded far down the fish's throat.

I took my plump Arctic grayling back to the camper, and smugly (but with a proper degree of modesty) showed it to Pauline, who looked at it and commented, "That's nice. But it's too big for our frying pan."

## Gamefish

Arctic grayling, Dolly Varden char, mountain whitefish.

## Seasons And Daily Catch Limits

### Grayling
Daily catch limit: two, but you must release all under 30 cm and you may keep only one over 45 cm. Possession: one daily catch limit. Tetsa River is closed to fishing April 1 to June 30.

### Dolly Varden Char
Daily catch limit: one. Possession limit: one. Tetsa River is closed to fishing April 1 to June 30. Open to fishing October 16 to March 31. Catch-and-release August 15 to October 15. Minimum length 30 cm. Maximum length 45 cm.

### Whitefish
Daily catch limit: fifteen fish. The Tetsa River is closed to fishing April to June 30.

For complete information on fishing regulations: www.bcfisheries.gov.bc.ca or phone B.C. Fish & Wildlife (250) 774-3547 or (250) 788-3611.

## Fly Fishing

### Flies for Grayling and Mountain Whitefish
- **Dry Flies:** number 12 to 22, March Brown, Tom Thumb, Humpy, Grey Wulff, Irresistible, Black Bivisible, Brown Bivisible, Black Gnat, Blue Dun.
- **Wet Flies:** number 8 to 14 Black Gnat, Coachman, Cowdung, Black Woolly Worm, March Brown, Montreal, Black Ant.

Tetsa River Provincial Campground.

### Lures for Dolly Varden
- Silver or red Krocodile, Dardevle, Koho, and Five of Diamonds spoons.

## Outfitters, Charters, River Tours

**Tetsa River Outfitters**
Box 238, Fort Nelson, BC V0C 1R0
Phone (250) 774-1005.
On Alaska Highway, Historic Mile 375 (new mileage 347).

## Fishing Tackle

**Tetsa River Outfitters**
(Historic Mile 375, new mileage 347)
Will have a minimal selection of fishing tackle. However, major items should be purchased in the town of Fort Nelson at Alaska Highway Mile 283.

# Accommodations

### Tetsa River Provincial Park
Alaska Highway, Mile 346
at the confluence of Mill Creek and Tetsa River.

### Tetsa River Outfitters
Historic mile 375 (new mileage 347).

Campground and lodge, gasoline and diesel fuel, souvenir items, fishing information and minimal tackle for the Tetsa River. Hiking tours and trail rides, outfitting and packing-in hunting parties. Photo shoots and fishing trips. Snacks—try Tetsa Outfitter's world-famous cinnamon buns, homemade bread and coffee.

## Highway Distances to the Tetsa River

From:

- Vancouver, BC - 1750 km. (1087 miles)
- Blaine WA, USA border crossing - 1743 km. (1083 miles)
- Calgary, AB - 1455 km. (903 miles)
- Edmonton, AB - 1175 km. (730 miles)

## Sikanni Chief River

Anglers may wish to check out the nearby Muskwa and Fort Nelson Rivers. Get info from Cliff Andrews at Tetsa outfitters or at tackle dealers and info center in Fort Nelson.

When you leave the Tetsa River and drive south on the Alaska Highway, here is a suggestion that may result in a couple of hours of worthwhile fly fishing. At Mile 162, park on the north side of the Sikanni Chief River. Take your fly rod and walk through the Sikanni River Lodge's campground to the river. Now stroll under the highway bridge and make a few casts from the downstream shore. The last time I was there, it didn't take long to nail a few legal-size Arctic grayling.

A word of warning: Usually there are hundreds of swallows' nests under the bridge deck and large swarms of swallows constantly swooping and pooping. If you walk along the riverbank under this bridge, maybe you should wear a broad-brimmed hat or carry an umbrella. Incidentally, the locals claim that early September is the best time for grayling fishing here.

Tiny Charlie Lake, a few miles north of Fort St. John on the Alaska Highway, offers excellent walleye fishing. This little body of water is within a stone's throw of the Alaska Highway.

# CHAPTER 6

# Quesnel River — A Likely Story

*The whole purpose of summer fishing is not just to worry about catching fish, but just to get out of the house and set and think a little.*

— ROBERT RUARK

I t was early in the morning on Saturday, June 28, 1997, in the city of Quesnel, British Columbia. The sun was shining brightly and all was well with the world as Pauline and I began our journey to the old Cariboo mining community of Likely at the headwaters of the Quesnel River for a week or two of trout fishing, camping, exploring and relaxing. The drinking water tank in our camper-van was bone dry, so we stopped at Quesnel's Tingley Park to fill up from the water faucet the city has provided for RV travelers. I connected our water tank hose to the faucet and, while filling our tank we discovered that Quesnel's water pressure was about a million pounds per square inch. The pressure blew our water tank apart at the seams. There was a small liquid explosion; our carpet and several cupboards were saturated, and a steady stream of water poured out the camper-van's doors.

After the initial shock, we disconnected the hose, left the park and drove along the highway south of town where we knew there were two RV supply stores. We had to buy a new water tank, but discovered we couldn't because the RV shops and many other businesses were closed for an extended Canada Day weekend. Canada's birthday, July 1, fell on a Tuesday, a situation which prompted many business folks to close their doors on the preceding Saturday, Sunday and

Gordon Davies and a Quesnel River Rainbow.

Patricia Brown with a three-pound-plus lake trout at our campsite on Quesnel River at Likely.

Monday, thus creating a four-day holiday. I guess you might say we had a four-day holiday ourselves, but it wasn't very exciting. We lived in our van on the parking lot of a supermarket until Wednesday morning. While we were parked in the grocery store lot, I devoted a lot of time to thinking of all the good things I had heard about the Quesnel River. Since I had never before fished this trout river, I was becoming a trifle anxious to get started. There is road access into many parts of this big river but, if you wish to see all of it, phone one of the guides or river tour operators listed at the end of this chapter.

Mark Maillot, an avid, experienced Cariboo Country trout fisher, had told me that he found fishing for big trout better in the Quesnel River than in the Blackwater River, a legendary Cariboo-Chilcotin rainbow trout stream. Another successful local fisherman disclosed to me the exact location of his "secret hole" on the Cariboo River, a large tributary of the Quesnel. And the boys at the Cariboo Fly and Tackle Shop in Quesnel suggested that we should head for the top end of the Quesnel River, near Likely, because it was a good bet for big trout.

On Wednesday morning we drove to an RV supply store and purchased a new water tank. For obvious reasons, we also bought a water pressure reducer and attached it to our water hose. Then off we went into the high hills and the headwaters of the Quesnel River. At the bridge over the upper river, we had our first glimpse of the top end of this noble waterway. It was wide, the water was clean, and the river appeared to be fishable almost everywhere. It looked very inviting and very promising. We crossed the bridge into Likely, a tiny village by anyone's standards, but located in what may be one of the prettiest spots on the planet. It sits right on the marge of the magnificent upper Quesnel River—a location selected, no doubt, by the River Gods. A short distance upriver from Likely is Quesnel Lake, the actual headwaters of the Quesnel River. The riverine community of Likely is named after Plato John Likely, a local gold miner in the early 1900s. In Likely, I asked some people, "Where is the nearest campground?"

"You'll have to drive several miles up that road," one of the locals answered, "to Quesnel Lake, to find a fishing resort or a campground. There aren't any in this town."

We were exceedingly disappointed by this turn of events, because we hadn't driven up to the river's headwaters just to park at a resort on a lake. As we were leaving Likely to head for the lake, Pauline spotted a damaged sign on the end of an outbuilding. "Stop!" she commanded. "Look at that sign. There are some letters missing, but I think it says 'Tourist Information'."

I parked at the side of the road and walked over to read the sign. There certainly were letters missing, but obviously it had once read 'Tourist Accommodation.' Then I saw three modest campsites with electric hookups, each site fronting on the river. They were on a large piece of property at the rear of a roomy riverside home with green lawns and a private boat dock. There was nobody at the house, so I walked across the street to a small building wherein was housed a combination laundromat, post office, tackle shop and propane sales. I asked the proprietress of the establishment, "Do you know anything about the three campsites over there?"

"Oh, yes," she answered. "The people in the house are friends of mine, and the lady will be home later tonight but you go pick a spot you like, and pull in. It's quite all right." We parked in the best spot in the mini-campground and stayed right there for eleven days.

Next morning I took a couple of cameras and hiked through town, shot some photos both above and below the bridge, and spotted one particular piece of water that really looked fishy to me. At our camper-van late that afternoon I picked up a fly rod and a light spinning outfit, intending to stroll down the river to the spot that had caught my eye. As I left the camper I called to Pauline, "I'm going downstream to fish for a while." I walked to the fishy-looking run I had seen earlier. I fired out a Mepps Spinner, and on my sixth or seventh cast I nailed a hard-fighting fish. I landed it-a sixteen-inch rainbow trout. Believe it or not, sixteen inches is the minimum legal length for trout in the Quesnel River! And the catch limit is one per day.

I kept the fish, then walked straight back to our campsite, where Pauline exclaimed, "I thought you were going fishing!" "I did go fishing," I replied, "and here's a trout for supper." I was acting pretty cocky as I showed off that fish, but the funny thing is that although we stayed eleven days, it was the first and last trout I caught that I could keep. I never got another one that measured sixteen inches or longer.

Our lovely little riverside campsite (and the other two sites) are on the property of Ted and Maureen Brown, a friendly, obliging couple who moved from the coast to Likely in 1993. Ted works at logging during the week, but tries to get out on the river and the lower end of Quesnel Lake as often as possible on weekends. Ted loves to fish but, when we were there, the diehard angler in the Brown family was his son Dale (eleven years old in 1997). When we were camping on the Browns' property, this keen young angler was not only an avid river fisher, he was also an incurable optimist. And why not? He seemed to hook as many trout as anyone.

About a mile upstream from Brown's house and campsites is the headwaters of the river, and the lower end of Quesnel Lake. Boaters from Likely often cruise up to the lake to troll for big trout.

The community of Likely is situated on the north shore of the Quesnel River, but there are a couple of houses on the south side. Early in our stay at Likely, I met a gent who not only had a vacation home across the river, but also had fished the Quesnel River and

Fly fishing the Quesnel River at Likely.

Quesnel Lake for forty years. He was a fund of information and very unselfishly shared much of his knowledge of the local fishing with me. He is an unusually modest (and perhaps a trifle shy) fellow, and he asked me to promise not to use his name in any published story. So I will call him Tommy Harrigan, simply because this is not his name.

One afternoon when Pauline and I were chatting with some members of Ted Brown's family at the riverside, Tommy's small boat pulled into shore; he stepped out and handed Pauline a four-pound live lake trout, saying, "Here's some meat for dinner. I just left the other side, and was heading across the river to Likely. I put a line out behind the boat, and started to troll a Gibbs Stewart spoon. I immediately hooked this small lake trout, and brought it in to you. I didn't even have time to kill it."

In 1964, Tommy Harrigan's father proved that there are some big fish in Quesnel Lake when he boated an incredible twenty-eight pound rainbow trout. Undoubtedly some larger ones may have been caught in this huge glacier-fed lake but, for my money, a twenty-eight pounder is one humungous rainbow! Another trophy rainbow, a twenty-five-pound specimen caught by fishing guide Henry Beckett in 1982, can be seen, stuffed and mounted, at Quesnel Lake Resort.

Known to top ten pounds, Dolly Varden char also reside in Quesnel Lake. Lake trout, sometimes exceeding thirty pounds, have provided unforgettable sport for heavy tackle trollers here. In addition to its scientific monicker, salvelinus namaycush, the lake trout has many other aliases: gray trout, mackinaw, humper, lake char, paperbelly, bank trout, siskowet and togue. Some of the popular lures for all the heavy-weight trout and char are: Apex Hot Spots, Lucky Louie plugs and Gibbs Stewart spoons.

As most anglers realize, people are inclined to talk about the largest fish from any particular body of water. Therefore it is wise to note that most of the trout and char caught in Quesnel Lake weigh between one and seven pounds.

Here is a bit of information for boaters. Cariboo's largest lake, the Quesnel, has over three hundred miles of wild, rugged, almost uninhabited shoreline. This magnificent waterway is approximately two thousand feet deep in spots; it is surrounded by spectacular, but foreboding, mountains that reach an altitude of eight thousand feet. At the west end of the lake, the Quesnel River begins a long journey to its mouth, but first it flows past the small and friendly community of Likely, one of the few remaining Cariboo Gold Rush settlements.

The little old Likely Hilton Hotel is the cultural center of the village of Likely. This vintage wood frame structure has a few rooms upstairs, but half of them appear to be in a constant state of resurrection. However, its location is incomparable. Like the entire half-dozen commercial establishments in downtown Likely, the hotel and its adjoining pub have a superb view of the glorious Quesnel River, the pride of the Cariboo.

The cafe in the Likely Hilton is the only eatery in town and, although it's not big nor fancy nor new, this rustic restaurant serves the world's finest homemade beef-and-barley soup. At lunch time one day, while I was fishing within a stone's throw of the village, I leaned my rod against the outside wall of the cafe and headed for the open door. A bright and chatty little girl was standing in the doorway. "My name is Annie," she said. "I'm six and I wanna be thirty, but I gotta be seven first."

Later that same day, as I was returning to our little campground, I decided to stop at the restaurant for a cup of coffee. The little gal was still at the door with the same line, "My name is Annie. I'm six and I wanna be thirty ..."

I think it was the great Art Linkletter who first uttered those oft-repeated words, "Kids say the darnedest things!"

While hiking around during our stay at Ted Brown's mini-campground, I found and fished some of the most-favored pools between the rapids (lower end of the lake) and the Likely Bridge, then downstream a considerable distance below the bridge. I cast wet flies, dry flies and weighted spinners, and got most of my hits on one-twelfth to one-eighth ounce weighted-body spinners. Except for that rainbow I caught on my first day here, all the trout I hooked were under the sixteen-inch minimum length. Que sera, sera.

Most common trout flies are effective on the upper Quesnel River. Grizzly King, Black Gnat, Woolly Worm and Coachman (and perhaps two hundred other wet flies) can attract the trout when they are feeding. Dry flies such as Tom Thumb, Humpy, Green Wulff, Adams, Mosquito and Iron Blue Dun are good bets when conditions are right. Downstream from the bridge you can often find good trout fishing at Murray's Pool (private property, ask permission), and the Bullion Pool, which can be fished properly only at low water. Most local folks can direct you to these well-known pools.

In the heart of Likely, on the north shore of the river, there is a broad expanse of green lawn that serves as a community picnic park, a helicopter pad and an extremely tiny Tourist Information Center (if and when there is a staff to operate it). Here also is a long, floating, wooden boat dock, upon which you'll frequently see fly casters laying out long lines to reach the best trout water. On the shoreline, from the boat dock downriver to the bridge, vegetation is scarce. There are no dense bushes to foul up your back casts; it's mostly grass, weeds, gravel and bare soil. Along this stretch I admired the flawless casts of an expert fly fisher who was offering a fly to a large group of steadily rising trout. I watched from a prudent distance and, although his casting (sometimes from a kneeling position) was flawless, I never saw him get a single strike, even though I followed the action all the way from the boat dock to the bridge.

For decades I had envied those fly fishermen who consistently made long, perfectly executed casts. But one day it occurred to me that the clumsy, blundering casters, such as I am, often catch just as many fish as the technically perfect experts do. After all, what benefit is there in being the greatest caster on the face of the globe if the trout won't take your fly?

Fly casting near Likely Bridge on Quesnel River.

Big fat chinook salmon (aka spring, king, tyee, quinnat) are the largest game fish available to Quesnel River sportsmen, but there are tight restrictions on fishing for chinooks. During the July to September spawning migration, when the government fisheries authorities believe the salmon are abundant, they announce special two- to six-week openings, but otherwise they are closed to angling. Currently (year 2002) the big chinook salmon are open to angling below Poquette Creek from July 15 to September 1. For anglers not familiar with saltwater fish, the chinook is the largest of all Pacific salmon.

Pauline and I drove eight miles northwest of Likely to the confluence of the Cariboo River (a large tributary) and the Quesnel River at the historic ghost town of Quesnel Forks. During the Cariboo Gold Rush in the early 1860s, Quesnel Forks (population five thousand) was the largest community on the mainland of British Columbia. In spite of serious damage to the old log buildings by massive mudslides, erosion and flooding in 1898, 1948 and 1996, some public-spirited citizens of Likely (including Dave Falconer and Jimbo Smith) are attempting to rescue and restore the deserted town of Quesnel Forks. If Jimbo and Dave succeed in their efforts, future generations will owe them a huge debt of gratitude for saving an important part of British Columbia's heritage.

Recent heavy rains had muddied the steep dirt road leading downhill into Quesnel Forks, so I parked at the top of the hill, where Pauline and I enjoyed a dramatic overview of the merging rivers and part of the old gold-mining town. We weren't surprised to find that the hill was muddy. While we were camping beside the Quesnel River on this July trip, we didn't see much summer weather—only two sunny days. Mostly we received thunder, lightning, cold winds, rain and hail. One night while sleeping in our van, we were awakened at three a.m. by heavy hailstones beating a tattoo on the roof. When we stepped outside in the morning, the ground was covered with two inches of unmelted hail. In July!

The Cariboo River, which flows into the Quesnel River at Quesnel Forks, offers good fishing for rainbow trout and fat Dolly Varden char. Access can be a problem except, perhaps, for those athletic anglers who canoe and portage downstream from Spectacle Lake or Bowron Lake (both north of Quesnel Forks).

Downriver from Likely and Quesnel Forks, the big Quesnel River meanders and snakes its way through some of the wildest, most scenic forested country in British Columbia. Wildlife abounds. Canada geese, ducks, loons, eagles, ospreys and grouse may be spotted almost anywhere. Moose, deer, caribou, mink, wolverines, black bears and grizzlies are fairly common. In fact, bears regularly venture into the outskirts of Likely, and occasionally wander right into the middle of the village.

Summertime brings a profusion of brightly-colored wildflowers to the Quesnel River Valley—fireweed, sweet clover, wild roses, several daisy-like flowers and dozens of other magnificent blooms that we horticulturally-illiterate anglers couldn't identify. Berry pickers can gather wild raspberries, huckleberries, Saskatoons and strawberries.

Quality trout fishing may be found in many locations throughout the length of the Quesnel River, but limited road access and posted private properties can sometimes prevent anglers from getting to streamside. However, halfway between Likely and the city of Quesnel, on the old Quesnel-Hydraulic Road, you'll find the free Beavermouth Forestry Campground. Here anglers have good access to the river at, and near, the mouth of Beaver Creek.

At the town of Quesnel, the big Quesnel River vanishes forever as it deposits all its flow into "Old Muddy," the wide, eight-hundred-mile-long Fraser River. In Quesnel, at the confluence of the Quesnel and Fraser rivers, there is a walking-hiking-strolling-cycling trail that will appeal to all river lovers. Aptly named the Riverfront Trail, this delightful and unique scenic pathway winds along six miles of the Fraser River, Quesnel River and Baker Creek shorelines, actually crossing the mighty Fraser on a footbridge at one point. There isn't a true river lover on earth who won't love hiking along this marvelous trail.

# What's where ?
## And where is what ?

## Gamefish Species

Rainbow trout, Dolly Varden, chinook salmon. Occasionally a two- to seven-pound lake trout moves into the upper river. Around the mouth of the Quesnel River almost any species is liable to move into the lower reaches from the Fraser River. The river is noted mainly for its fine—often large—rainbow trout.

## Angling Methods

### Fly fishing

This is a fine fly-fishing river throughout most of its length. At one time or another, the rainbow trout will hit almost any fly known to mortal man, but standard wet fly patterns usually will produce: wet flies such as Black Gnat, Royal Coachman, Woolly Worm, Grizzly King and Coachman are all good bets. For dry patterns you won't go far wrong with Adams, Humpy, Mosquito, Lady McConnell, Iron Blue Dun and Tom Thumb.

Phone Cariboo Fly and Tackle in the town of Quesnel for more suggestions, (250) 747-3273.

**Trolling (Quesnel Lake)**

Lucky Louie plugs, Apex Hot Spots, Gibb's Stewart spoons.

**Spinning**

For rainbow trout and Dolly Varden char: weighted spinners such as Mepps in small and medium sizes. Flatfish plugs (smallish), small wobbling spoons including silver Krocodiles

For chinook salmon: large spoons, such as Gibbs Koho Spoon, Stewart Spoon, Kitimat Spoon, Krocodile Spoon, Wiggle Wart Plug and Hottentot Plug.

# Restrictions and Regulations

- Minimum length trout and Dolly Varden char: 40 cm (15 3/4 inches). Catch limit for trout and char: one per day.
- Chinook salmon: downstream from Poquette Creek — open July 15 to September 1. Chinook daily catch limit: 4 chinook per day, but only 2 may be 50 cm. Bait ban.
- Quesnel River open to fishing (above mouth of tributary Cariboo River) June 16 to February 28. Below mouth of Cariboo River open July 1 to March 31.
- No fishing from 50 meters above Likely Bridge to 50 meters below Likely Bridge.
- Because of the possibility of sudden closures, anglers should contact government fisheries for information. Phone (250) 992-4212 or (250) 398-4530. and/or visit the BC Fisheries web site: www.bcfisheries.gov.bc.ca

# Guides, Outfitters, Charters, River Tours

**Steve Beedle**
1481 Lakeview Crescent, Quesnel, BC, Canada V2J 4J8
Phone (250) 747-5201

Steve Beedle is a licensed fishing guide who really knows the Quesnel River. This accomplished fly fisher will take you to the finest trout waters along the big river.

**Cariboo Mountain Outfitters**
Box 4010, Quesnel BC, Canada V2J 3J2
Phone (250) 747-3334, Fax (250) 747-3120

Bradley Bowden uses a 20-foot jet boat with a 350 HP motor for his guided tours on the Quesnel River. In a single day in the autumn of 2000, Brad spotted nine bears along the river.

## Tackle Shops

**Cariboo Fly and Tackle**
1196 Chew Road, Quesnel, BC, Canada V2J 4E1
Phone (250) 747-3273

## Accommodations

**Gold Pan Motel**
855 Front Street, Quesnel, BC V2J 2L3
Phone (250) 992-2107

**Fraser Bridge Inn**
100 Ewing Avenue, Quesnel, BC  V2J 2L3
Phone (250) 992-5860

**Morehead Lake Resort on Likely Road**
Mailing address: PO Box 136, Likely, BC, Canada V0L 1N0
Phone (250) 790-2323

**Ted Brown's**
little campground on the river in the village of Likely
Phone (250) 790-2557

# Distances to the Quesnel River

**From:**

- Vancouver, BC - 660 km (369 miles)
- Blaine, WA. USA border - 650 km (364 miles)
- Calgary, AB - 900 km (540 miles)
- Edmonton, AB - 850 km (510 miles)

Anglers who are interested in large fish may wish to do some trolling on big Quesnel Lake at the headwaters of the Quesnel River. There have been 24- to 28-pound trout caught here by trolling sportfishers. Cariboo Fly and Tackle in the city of Quesnel can give you detailed information on this rather remote, famous lake. Phone 250-747-3273.

Another worthwhile area for lakes and streams is the Barkerville-Wells-Bowron Lake area, reached via Highway 26 east from the City of Quesnel.

CHAPTER 7

# Blackwater River 200 Years After Alex Mackenzie

*It strikes me that, in the hi-tech world in which we live, fishing has*
*become increasingly important to ensure we hang on to our sense*
*of values.*

— SANDY LEVENTON
editor, *Trout and Salmon Magazine*
United Kingdom, August, 1996

I n the summer of 1793, along the big, uncharted Fraser River, near
the present-day city of Quesnel, the dedicated and unstoppable
Scottish explorer Alexander Mackenzie steered his canoe into the
mouth of the Blackwater River. With his assistant Alex McKay, two
Indian guides, six voyageurs from Quebec and a dog, Mackenzie
was determined to be the first paleface to cross the entire North
American continent from the Atlantic Ocean to the Pacific Ocean.

As they traveled westward through the valley of the Blackwater
and its tributaries, the adventurous Scot and his companions were
beginning the last leg of an incredible journey. Working for the North
West Company, a giant in the North American fur trade, Alexander
Mackenzie's job was to explore new trade routes, establish trading
posts and, on this present journey, to search for a possible overland
route to a Pacific seaport.

Mackenzie began his historic trek on the Atlantic coast of Canada
at the mouth of the St. Lawrence River. Crossing the great unknown
continent in the 1700s was an undertaking of considerable magni-
tude. There were no railroads, no highways, no automobiles, no
motels—not even a commercial airline. For Alexander's rag-tag

band, it was all foot-slogging, canoe-paddling, portaging and ford-ing. Across eastern Canada and the endless barren prairies went the ten brave trailblazers. Upon reaching the Rocky Mountains, they faced the unknown. Beyond the Rockies they knew only that they must head west if they were ever to find the western sea. By what route, through what perils, for what distance, they knew not. But Alexander the Great knew exactly how to reach the Pacific shores. He did what he'd always done on his previous explorations. He trust-ed the local people. Passing from tribe to tribe, he befriended the native North American inhabitants and followed their advice and directions without question.

Fraser River Indians led Mackenzie's group to the mouth of the Blackwater River, hence, up the Euchiniko and Blackwater valleys, and westward to the sea near Bella Coola. There, Alex mixed grease with vermilion pigment and painted upon a large flat-faced rock, "ALEXANDER MACKENZIE FROM CANADA BY LAND, JULY 22, 1793."

The old river worshipper, Gordon Davies, playing rainbow trout near Batnuni Road Bridge.

Blackwater River near Quesnel.

This doesn't read like a Hollywood Indian shoot-em-up script, and it is a fact that on none of Mackenzie's North American explorations did any member of his crew ever fire a shot in anger. Yet, incredibly, he always brought all his companions back alive. You were one helluva man, Mr. Mackenzie!

The Blackwater (alias West Road) River flows eastward from the boundary of Tweedsmuir Park in central British Columbia, then slips into and out of Basalt, Eliguk, Tsacha, Euchiniko and Kluskoil lakes. The Blackwater Valley is the home of moose, bears, beavers, otters, mink, bald eagles, ospreys, loons, sandhill cranes and, occasionally, white pelicans flying to and from their Chilcotin breeding grounds. But the most important species of animal, fish or fowl found here is the famous Blackwater race of wild rainbow trout that can dish up top-notch, heart-stopping action for anglers. Gorging themselves on an abundance of mayflies, caddisflies, stone flies and a variety of other insects, these resident rainbows grow up healthy, hardy, fat and feisty.

The Blackwater River is renowned far and wide for its famous "Blackwater strain" of wild rainbow trout. Although an angler may hook a whitefish, Dolly Varden char or a squawfish, in this tributary of the big Fraser River these species are of little consequence, because the Blackwater is first, last and always, a wild rainbow waterway. No hatchery trout!

Kluskoil Lake is at the downstream end of a long chain of lakes along the upper Blackwater River. This body of water is best reached by float planes provided by some North Cariboo fishing lodges, resorts or guide services. Above Kluskoil Lake, the river is rather small; not too deep for wading, and it's a simple matter to reach all the water with an easy cast. Downriver from Kluskoil Lake, drift boat fishing with a guide can give an angler some exceptional fly-fishing. Visiting fishers have commented on these guided float trips: "…dozens of rainbows on dry flies every day." "It's like the Yellowstone River a hundred years ago " "…the fishing trip of a lifetime!"

Some fly-fishers claim they have caught twenty-five-inch rainbows in this fine stream that has no hatchery trout (all wild) in its waters. The Blackwater holds plenty of rainbow trout, but most of this waterway is accessible by road in very few places. Unless a visiting angler has several weeks and a good riverboat, he'd better hire an experienced local guide if he wishes to hook some sizeable trout. Guide David Harrington at Harrington's Hideaway on Euchiniko Lakes Ranch will take you to where the large rainbow trout are. See the "What's Where" section for his phone number.

A major tributary, the Nazko River, flows in from the south, then the Blackwater takes a turn to the left and heads northward to Gillies Crossing and the mouth of the Euchiniko River. This is a popular spot for some locals who launch their boats here for downriver drifting. It is wilderness fishing, drifting mile after mile through the evergreen forest—and the rainbow trout are numerous. There are gravel beaches along the way that allow the drift fishers to beach their boats and cast from shore. Below Gillies Crossing, the Batnuni Road Bridge crosses the Blackwater River. On either side of the bridge a fly caster can reach some fine fish-holding water by hiking along the gravel, sand and rocks at streamside. But when the river is bank-high and the current is strong, it's almost impossible to walk more than a couple of hundred yards upriver or downriver from the bridge.

Following a heavy rain in July 1996, I was fishing a dry fly near this bridge during high water. The stream was clean and clear, but walking through the bushes along the riverbank was inconvenient and more than somewhat treacherous, so I was forced to stay at the heavily-fished water near the bridge. I nailed a few smallish trout, released them, and then walked across the bridge to shoot some photos of a fly caster who introduced himself as Dave Butt of Quesnel. Dave said he had been casting to some feeding rainbows but hadn't been able to interest them in his artificials.

He pointed downriver a short distance to a lady fly caster, and said, "That's my wife Bev, and she just released a twelve-inch trout and a whitefish, but I haven't been able to hook even one fish!"

Bev stopped casting and started to wade toward us. When she walked up to us, I greeted her with, "Dave tells me you've been out-fishing both of us."

Dave looked a mite sheepish when Bev replied, "But did Dave mention that this is the first time I ever used a fly rod?"

The Blackwater is a fine fly-fishing stream. It would be foolish to claim that certain fly patterns are guaranteed to work all the time, but nonetheless here are some popular Blackwater patterns: Muddler Minnow, Coachman, Doc Spratley, Humpy, Irresistible, Tom Thumb, Elk Hair Caddis and other caddisfly patterns. Some Blackwater fly fishers use caddisflies almost exclusively, with astonishing results.

A scenic canyon area on the lower river is easily accessible at the Blackwater Crossing Bridge on the old Blackwater Road. There is a dramatic rock-walled canyon here, a very large pool immediately below the bridge, and campgrounds on both sides of the bridge. For a shore-bound wading angler this is one of the most accessible sections of the entire Blackwater River. Below Blackwater Crossing, heading in an easterly direction, the noble waterway meanders, surges and races, then empties its clear, clean waters into the muddy Fraser River near the little community of Strathnaver.

We cannot leave the Blackwater without a visit to a couple of major tributaries that offer serious sport for fly-fishermen: the Nazko River and the Euchiniko River.

## Tributary — Euchiniko River

Near its mouth, the Euchiniko River widens, then empties into the Blackwater at Gillies Crossing. Although there is some fairly good fly-fishing for trout in the Euchiniko, its main claim to fame is that it drains a long string of popular rainbow trout lakes. From Gillies Crossing my wife Pauline and I drove up the Euchiniko River on dirty, dusty, lumpy Batnuni Road, then along a side road to pretty Pelican Lake. The fairly large Forestry campground at Pelican Lake was almost totally deserted, although it was midsummer when we were there. Gang trolls and worms are used by many anglers on this lake, but fly-fishing can also be effective. One- to two-pounders can be caught at Pelican, but most of the trout are smaller.

Leaving Pelican Lake we drove west along Batnuni Road and the Euchiniko River to long, narrow Titetown Lake. There are rainbow trout here and Dolly Varden char too; some of these Dollies will top three pounds in weight. A hop-skip-and-a-jump west of Titetown is Boat Lake, a small but good fly-fishing spot with boat launching facilities and inexpensive campsites. We left Boat Lake and camped overnight at Hanham Lake. This smallish body of water has a Forestry Service campground, primitive launching facilities for small cartop or inflatable craft, and quite good fly fishing and spinning for rainbows and Dollies. The Euchiniko River below Hanham Lake is worth a try for Dolly Varden and trout. Another short drive along the rocky road brought us to lovely Batnuni Lake, the jewel of the Euchiniko Valley. We drove into Batnuni Resort to admire the panoramic view of the lake from the main lodge building and to visit with the friendly proprietors and staff.

Situated on the lakeshore, this homey resort has a float plane dock, boat and motor rentals, launching ramp, smokehouse, hot showers, cabins, campsites, home-cooked meals, a licensed bar in the lodge and professional fishing guides. In addition to all this, Batnuni Resort operates fly-in fishing trips to Kluskoil Lake and the upper Blackwater River. Batnuni's rainbow trout have been known to tip the scales at three pounds, but one pound is a more usual weight. Fly fishing for these wild native trout is often best in the shallows around the islands. The lake also has populations of kokanee, lake trout and Dolly Varden.

For outdoor types who enjoy primitive camping there are two Forestry Service campgrounds on the lake.

## Tributary — Nazko River

When I first laid eyes on the famous Blackwater River I knew for certain I was gazing upon a noble, classic rainbow trout river. But I must admit I had a similar feeling when I saw its tributary, the Nazko River, for the first time. Smaller than the Blackwater, the Nazko is big enough

to hold robust rainbow trout of over two pounds in weight, and there's plenty of insect life along the stream to fatten up a large trout population. In addition, the Nazko is a truly lovely little wild river.

The village of Nazko, on the Nazko River, is extremely small but it boasts a good little restaurant, a store with a fair supply of basic groceries, a modern laundromat, gasoline pumps, propane sales, and a campground. From Nazko Village, a gravel road follows the Nazko River in a northerly direction, past the Indian community of Nahooja, through green pine and aspen forest, alongside old snake fences, a few log structures, pasture land with great expanses of white daisies, and an occasional glimpse of the river. We drove along this narrow, dusty track, winding uphill and down, past prolific wild roses, Indian paintbrush, red fireweed and diminutive not-too-sweet wild strawberries, until we came to the junction of the Nazko and Blackwater rivers.

On the main road south of the hamlet of Nazko, right at the edge of town, a bridge crosses the Nazko River. The water was high but clean, so I fished here for a short time, both upstream and downstream of the bridge. On my first cast I had a hard strike from a rather small trout. Surprisingly, the fish smacked my floating Tom Thumb fly as noisily as a fish five times its size. In no time at all I had half-a-dozen more strikes. I released all the fish I hooked. They were only eight to eleven inches long, but they were fat, healthy, rosy-sided rainbows. Near this bridge, a gravel thoroughfare with the unlikely name of Honolulu Road runs southward, paralleling the Nazko River (upstream) for about twelve miles before it crosses the stream at a bridge, providing access for anglers.

We camped for a couple of nights at tiny Marmot Lake on the outskirts of the village of Nazko. Marmot truly is a surprising little body of water. A total of forty thousand rainbow trout were planted here and this stocking program paid off handsomely. Anglers with cartop boats were catching one- to two-pound trout with fair regularity by trolling, fly fishing and spinning. Scenic little Marmot Lake is surrounded by thick bush, but there's a well-beaten path around the shoreline for hikers and bank fishers.

One of these days I hope to re-visit the Blackwater, the Nazko and the Euchiniko rivers, and spend a lot more time fishing and a lot less

*Opposite:* Nazko River, lovely fishy, tributary of Blackwater near confluence.

time exploring and photographing. Offhand I cannot imagine a more appealing rainbow trout region than the valleys of the Blackwater and its tributaries. From what I've seen I have a hunch mid-August would be the ideal time for my return trip.

Trout fishing in the Blackwater Valley is outstanding today at the beginning of the new millennium, but it must have been awesome two hundred years ago when Alexander Mackenzie was here and remarked on the abundance of trout and salmon. If Mackenzie and his merry men had been river anglers rather than fur traders, I'll bet they never would have left the Blackwater Valley.

# What's where ?
## And where is what ?

## Gamefish Species

### The Famous Fighting Blackwater Rainbow Trout

Fly fishing for the healthy, handsome Blackwater rainbows is the name of the game here! On the Blackwater River you should forget all about the mountain whitefish, Dolly Varden char and the seasonal salmon spawning run (closed to fishing anyway). Just concentrate on the famous, lovely acrobatic Blackwater rainbow trout that reach lengths of over two feet.

## Restrictions

- Single barbless hook. Single artificial fly only.
- Mainstem of the river is closed to fishing November 1 to June 14. Tributaries of the Blackwater are closed April 1 to June 30.
- All salmon are totally closed to fishing. Minimum size is 30 cm (11 7/8 inches).
- Boats: electric motors only.

- **Note: this is a class 2 classified water.** An angler must purchase a Class 2 licence in addition to a basic angling licence. For further information on angling regulations. Phone (250) 992-4212 or (250) 398-4530, or visit the B.C. Fisheries web site: www.bcfisheries. gov.bc.ca

## Flies

Check with local tackle shop, fishing guides and local anglers, then stock up on the flies they recommend.

But take along all your river-fishing trout flies, particularly standard patterns such as Muddler Minnow, Elk Hair Caddis, Irresistible, Humpy, Tom Thumb, Doc Spratley, Carey Special, Black Ant, Mosquito, Coachman. It would be wise to take all the caddisfly patterns you can, because these patterns are extremely popular on the Blackwater.

## Fishing Guides

**David Harrington**
Euchiniko Lakes Ranch
Box 2509, Vanderhoof, BC V0J 3A0
Phone (250) 567-4939

David guides anglers on only one river system—the Blackwater and its tributaries. He can take you to all the spots where the rainbows are hiding out.

## Tackle Shop

Cariboo Fly and Tackle
1196 Chew Road, Quesnel, BC, V2J 4E
Phone (250) 747-3273

They have best fly patterns for the Blackwater

# Accommodations

**Harrington's Hideaway** — right on the river
Box 2509, Vanderhoof, BC V0J 3A0
Phone (250) 567-4939

**Fishpot Lake Resort**
(Near Nazko, BC, on tributary of Blackwater). This lake has
rainbows to 4 pounds (average 9 to 15 inches).
Phone (250) 992-5860 ext. 900

**Fraser Bridge Inn and RV Park**
100 Ewing Ave., Quesnel, BC V2J 1R4
Phone (250) 992-5860

# Highway Distances to the Blackwater River

**From:**

- Vancouver, BC — 735 km (456 miles)
- Blaine, WA, USA border — 728 km (452 miles)
- Calgary, AB — 975 km (605 miles)
- Edmonton, AB — 925 km (574 miles)

# CHAPTER 8

# Red Hot Pinks at Bella Coola
plus the Atnarko River

*Fishing is a delusion, entirely surrounded by liars in old clothes.*

— DON MARQUIS

O n July 21, 1997, our friends Fred and Penny Patrick drove their camper-van from Gibson's Landing up to Williams Lake to meet Pauline and me. Together we drove our vans across the Freedom Road (Highway 20) to Anahim Lake and from there down the mountain to the Bella Coola River on August 2. For the next two weeks we caught and released dozens of shiny-bright, fresh-from-the-sea, scrappy pink salmon. We released most of the fish, keeping only a few for the pot. At dinnertime every day we dined on pink salmon. Penny, Pauline and Fred cooked and served baked pink salmon, fried pink salmon, broiled pink salmon and teriyaki salmon fillets. I had read somewhere that a seafood chef can flake the cooked pink salmon meat for a great salmon soufflé, but none of our three cooks would try this.

Our timing for the arrival of the pink salmon run was perfect. The pinks were there in large numbers and in excellent condition from the day we arrived until we left on August 16. Before you get the impression that we were clever enough to know exactly when the fish would arrive in the river, let me set the record straight. Earlier in the year, Fred had asked me to find out when the pinks would be arriving in the Bella Coola River, so we could be there at the optimum time.

"Of course," I said, "I'll be in Williams Lake at the end of June,

West coast angler Fred Patrick with pink salmon at Bella Coola River (Hagensborg).

Early on a summer evening on Bella Coola River near Airport Pool.

and I'll talk to the fisheries people there. Then I'll phone and give you the info."

I didn't expect any problems, but perhaps I should have!

Pauline and I arrived in Williams Lake on June 24. Upon learning that there was a fisheries office in Room 401 of a new government building, I hastened to the office building, punched the number four in the elevator, rode up, and stepped out of the elevator into what I expected would be a hallway. It wasn't—I was in an office. As I turned around, looking for a door to a hall, I heard a pleasant female voice behind me, inquiring "May I help you?" I turned around and saw an attractive young woman behind a counter.

I stammered, "Somehow I stepped out of the elevator into your office instead of the hallway. Where is the hall?"

"Oh," she said brightly. "There isn't one. As part of its economy drive, the government is constructing buildings without halls because they're a waste of space. And soon, as part of our economy drive, we'll only speak to members of the public between ten a.m. and three p.m."

Confused, I mumbled, "Excuse me, ma'am, but I was just looking for a little information on pink salmon in the Bella Coola River."

"Well, you're in the right place," she said. "but I'm afraid there's nobody here today who could assist you. I'll give you some names and phone numbers that you can call to find the information." She really was trying to be helpful.

I left the building with a long list of names of Fish and Wildlife experts, Federal Fisheries folks, and other fishery authorities, with phone numbers and addresses from Williams Lake to Bella Coola. For the next couple of weeks, between the city of Quesnel and the village of Likely, up and down the Quesnel River, whenever I was near a pay phone, I called the telephone numbers on the list. I reached receptionists who said the experts were out of town, I reached answering machines, and a few times I got no answers at all to my calls. I soon learned to call person-to-person. This did save me money, but I never got through to anyone who could answer my simple question, "When does the pink salmon run usually enter the Bella Coola River?" I was a mite worried because I'd promised Fred I would phone and tell him when to meet us, so we could drive together to Bella Coola.

From a small, rustic cafe in Likely's little old hotel, fifteen days after I'd started phoning, I was trying to place a person-to-person call to anyone on my list. The exercise was a total failure, and I even found myself explaining the entire debacle to the telephone operator. I guess the half dozen patrons in the restaurant must have heard my frustrated pleas on the pay phone because, as I hung up, a gentleman walked over and said, "I couldn't help overhearing your conversation. If you'll phone the Kopas Store in Bella Coola you'll get all the information you require."

I gave the kind man a hearty "thank you," called the Kopas Store and spoke to manager John Morton, who said, "August 1 is the best time to start fishing for pink salmon." I called Fred Patrick and gave him the August 1 date. As it turned out, our Bella Coola pink salmon fishing trip was an absolutely spectacular success.

And, in fairness to all government fisheries people, I must confess that when I had been in the Bella Coola Valley for a week I met a gent named Lyle Enderud, of the federal Department of Fisheries and Oceans, who was exceedingly helpful, providing me with piles of statistical information when I asked for help.

Here's some info on the timing of the Bella Coola spawning runs, based mainly on statistics from Lyle: pink salmon begin to move into the Bella Coola River in July, but the real hot-and-heavy angling for pinks usually doesn't occur until early in August. Occasionally, fishing can remain fairly good until late August. The vanguard of the pink salmon run moves into the lower river between July 15 and July 25. Pinks (aka humpbacks or humpies) commonly weigh between three and five pounds, but some we encountered in 1997 on the Bella Coola weighed five to six pounds—a respectable weight, unless you compare it to the twelve-pound nine-ounce specimen that was caught in the Kenai River, Alaska, in 1974.

Chum (alias keta, dog) salmon are in the river at the same time as the pinks, and they are now legal game fish in the Bella Coola system. Unfortunately, it's hard to find really clean chum salmon in fresh water because they lose their silvery color and acquire rather ugly grid-like black bars when they enter the river. Best timing for chinook salmon can be between June 20 and July 8, but these big fish are present in the river from late May to mid-July. The chinooks attract fairly large crowds, and elbow-to-elbow fishing can occur at the most popular pools. Mid-September is usually the ideal time for coho salmon fishing, if there is an opening. Currently (as of the year 2002) there is a total closure on steelhead fishing. There is a limited opening on Dolly Varden char and cutthroat trout. If a large enough run of coho salmon appears (mid-September), openings may be announced.

I realize that most resident BC river fishers should be able to hook plenty of pink salmon without the assistance of fishing guides, but I believe most of us can benefit from the professional help of guides when seeking other species. Ken Corbould, Dean Emslie and Darwin Unrau are qualified local guides. All were recommended by a retired Bella Coola guide—and you will find their phone numbers in the lists of specs following this chapter.

Along the lower twelve miles of the Bella Coola River, between Hagensborg and the mouth, there are enough good pools to satisfy the desires of all anglers: the Ball Park Pool, the Airport Run, the mouth of the Saloompt River and the Bailey Bridge Pool. We poked around the river a little, but always gravitated back to the Bailey Bridge where fish were plentiful, the pool was easy to fish, and the rustic private campground on the river was simply too convenient to resist. The friendly, obliging camp management made camping there a total pleasure.

On our first day at the Bailey Bridge, Pauline, Fred and I soon had two pink salmon apiece. Penny wasn't fishing. She didn't have a licence, and had never even fished in a river. Watching all the action

Angler playing pink salmon at Bailey bridge.

Gordon at Bailey Bridge Pool, Bella Coola River.

made her a mite jealous, and she mentioned this to the camp manager. "In an hour," said the camp boss, "I'll be driving into town. Come with me and get yourself a fishing licence."

When Penny arrived with her licence, Fred set up a rod for her and on her second cast she nailed a pink that was bigger than any Fred or Pauline or I had caught. Then, next morning, she beached a clean nine-pound chum salmon (open to sportfishing) that we took to be smoked at the local seafood emporium, handily located on the tributary Saloompt River near the Bailey Bridge. I learned a lesson at the smoke house. The experts there told me that one cannot judge whether or not a chum salmon is suitable for smoking simply by looking at the exterior of the fish. You must cut into the flesh. If the meat still retains some pink color it is okay; if the meat is white it isn't suitable. Penny's fish was just fine.

When we started fishing the Bella Coola, we used specialized pink salmon flies, namely Johnny Carlson's Pink Fly, Hoochie, Pink Eve and others. We also had some other assorted red-and-white streamers. All of these flies worked well on the pink salmon, but after a couple of days, we realized that anglers using fluorescent yarn knotted onto a bare hook were catching as many fish as we were. Scarlet red was popular, but dark red, bright pink, orange or green fluorescent wool proved to be just as productive. We switched from our two-dollar flies to the one-penny wool.

Extremely short casts were sufficient because the salmon were holding in water between fifteen and forty feet off the gravel beach. Fly rods with sinking tips were ideal for this fishing but lightweight spinning tackle, with split shot on the leader, also worked perfectly.

Paul Araki of Kelowna, BC, was camping at the Bailey Bridge, and he put on an impressive exhibition of fly fishing for pink salmon. He didn't actually hook a fish on every cast, but he came about as close to doing it as anyone could. He was on the river almost all the time, day after day, beaching and releasing pinks and, at one point, he landed and put back a twenty-pound chum salmon—an exceptional feat considering the fast water at the lower end of the pool. Paul spent a considerable amount of time helping some of the young kids who were experiencing difficulties in casting, hooking and beaching fish. The youngsters noticed that he had a large supply of fluorescent yarn (and probably hooks too) so they knew whom to ask when they needed any minor fishing tackle items.

Paul Araki left the Bailey Bridge Campground a few days before we did. Then Fred Patrick, along with an enthusiastic Australian angler, Warren Watts (both these guys were catching and releasing vast numbers of fish) became the local experts who helped the kids and newcomers.

My own personal claim to fame at the Bailey Bridge was that I earned the title "Old Guy Who Fell Over the Big Rock." Actually it was a rather acrobatic feat—an outstanding example of athleticism, you might say. Standing at the water's edge on the gently sloping gravel beach, almost directly under the Bailey Bridge, I hooked a respectable-sized pink salmon. As I worked the fish in close to the shore, I took a couple of steps backward to slide it out onto the beach. I forgot there was a large boulder right behind me, and I did a graceful backward semi-somersault over the chunk of stone. Strange as it may seem, I held onto the rod and kept a tight line on the fish. I stood up and beached it—and it was a big one. The only physical damage I suffered was a minor scrape on one arm.

The rugged wilderness that is the mid-coast region of British

The big Fisheries Pool, near confluence of Atnarko and Talchako.

Columbia, which includes the entire Bella Coola Valley and the wild forests to the north and south, is the home of grizzlies, black bears (including the white Kermode strain), moose, deer, sea otters, beavers, marbled murrelets, goshawks, seagulls and a large population of bald eagles, but very few human beings. In fact, the population of the entire region is four thousand people, with twenty-six hundred of them living in the Bella Coola Valley.

We fished a good stretch of river near the airport at Hagensborg one day, then camped at the end of the airport and visited the same water the following morning. I spent most of the time there shooting photos, while Fred and Penny caught and released some nice pink salmon and a couple of chums. Here we met high school teacher Tony Burton who was fishing there with spinning tackle. He beached one pink salmon and hooked another fish that ran out most of his line before it broke off, leaving only seventeen feet of monofilament on his reel spool. Not many anglers would carry on fishing under this handicap, but Tony did. Miraculously, he hooked and landed a monster six-pound pink with the short piece of line left on his reel!

But that ain't all!

The following morning, fishing fanatic Tony Burton was back on the river, and his spool was filled with new line. Believe it or not, a heavy chum salmon ran out all his monofilament and broke it off at the reel. The last I heard, he was once again heading into town to buy more line.

Read on for a smidgeon of fascinating local history.

The majestic Bella Coola River is a big turquoise-colored water-way formed by the junction of the Atnarko and Talchako rivers near Stuie, BC. The Bella Coola flows westward through a lush, green, fifty-mile-long valley, flanked by massive glacier-laden alpine peaks, then empties into the eastern end of a snowcapped, mountain-bordered fiord at Bella Coola Harbor.

Visitors to the Bella Coola Valley might be curious about the preponderance of Norwegian names in the area. There is a very simple explanation for this. In the early 1890s a severe economic depression struck the northeastern United States. In Minnesota, the congregation of a Lutheran church, mostly Norwegian farmers, sent their pastor, Reverend Christian Saugstad, to the wild Pacific Northwest to find a site for a new settlement where they could perhaps escape from their starvation existence.

Among several places Saugstad investigated was the Bella Coola Valley. He traveled up and down the Bella Coola River in Indian canoes, and liked what he saw. The Reverend went to Victoria where the government told him that if he could establish a colony of at least thirty families, a wagon road through the river valley would be built for them, and each family would be given a gift of a hundred and sixty acres of land.

Back in Minnesota, Reverend Saugstad reported to his congregation: "In this Bella Coola Valley, you have many features of your beloved homeland of Norway. You approach it up a long fiord on both sides of which the mountains rise up almost perpendicularly to heights of six or seven thousand feet. Everywhere streams leap down the mountainsides and glaciers gleam in the sun. When you get into the valley proper, you walk through forests of tall stately fir and spruce. Game is abundant and the streams are never still from the splashing of fish."

The Norwegian congregation voted to move to Bella Coola. Seventy-nine families went, and the local folks tell me there are nine hundred descendants of the original Minnesota-Norwegians still living in the valley.

# What's where ?
# And where is what ?

## Gamefish Species
Chinook salmon, coho salmon, pink salmon, chum salmon, sockeye salmon, steelhead, cutthroat trout, Dolly Varden char.

## Regulations & Restrictions
- Chinook salmon open to fishing / 4 per day, but only one over 65 cm.
- Pink salmon open / 2 per day
- Chum salmon open / 1 per day
- Sockeye salmon closed to fishing.
- Steelhead closed to fishing.
- Cutthroat trout open in mainstem river only.
- Single barbless hook all year-round.

For updates on regulations, phone (250) 799-5345 or (250) 982-2421. Also: British Columbia Fisheries web site: www.bcfisheries.gov.bc.ca

# Bait, Lures and Flies

Note: There is a bait ban from Sept. 1 to May 15.

- **Chinook Salmon:** Natural baits including salmon eggs, Spin-n-Glo and other drift lures, Kitimat Spoon, large size Gibbs Koho Spoons. Krocodile wobbling spoons.

- Coho Salmon: Ghost shrimp, dew worms (nightcrawlers), salmon eggs, Gibbs Koho spoons. Coho flies: Clouser, Minnow, Pearl Mickey Finn, Coho Blue, Coho Peacock.

- Pink Salmon and Chum Salmon Flies: Red Handlebar, Hoochie, Pink Eve, Penner's Pink Fly, any bright pink, red or orange fly tied on a number 10 to 16 hook. Also bright pink yarn tied on a bare number 12 hook.

- Cutthroat Trout Flies: Silver Minnow, Woolly Worm, Black Gnat, Coachman, and all other west coast common wet fly and nymph patterns.

- Lures: Small size Mepps and other weighted spinners.

- Baits: Salmon eggs, ghost shrimp, dew worms (nightcrawlers).

- Dolly Varden Char: Dardevle spoons, Five of Diamonds spoons, Koho spoons, Mepps weighted spinners, salmon eggs, ghost shrimp or dew worms, leadhead jigs with "bubble gum pink" plastic wiggle bodies.


# Fishing Guides

Here are three first-rate, highly recommended, experienced fishing guides for the Bella Coola River:

- Darwin Unrau: Phone (250) 982-2633
- Dean Emslie: Phone (250) 982-2470
- Ken Carbould: Phone (250) 982-2477


# Tackle Shops

Kopas Store's fishing tackle department, (John Morton, Manager), in downtown Bella Coola. The Kopas Store is almost as old as the Village of Bella Coola. It is a fascinating little mini-department store with, among many other items, a good stock of fishing tackle for angling in the local waters. The store's boss man John is too modest to admit it, but he is a good source of information on the fishing in the Bella Coola Valley. Phone (250) 799-5553.

## Accommodations

**Bailey Bridge Campsite** on Saloompt River Road, Hagensborg
Box 552, Hagensborg, BC, Canada V0T 1H0
Phone (250) 982-2342

**Hagen Haven RV Park & Campground**
(on Highway 20 at Thorsen Creek)
Box 471, Bella Coola, BC, Canada V0T 1C0
Phone (250) 799-5659
No pets or credit cards

**Bella Coola Motel** on Clayton Street
Box 188, Bella Coola, BC, Canada V0T 1C0
Phone (250) 799-5323

**Bella Coola Valley Inn** on Mackenzie Street
Box 183, Bella Coola, BC, Canada V0T 1C0
Phone (250) 799-5316

**Bay Motor Hotel**
Box 216, Bella Coola, BC, Canada V0T 1C0
Phone toll free 1-888-982-2212

**Gnome's Home Campground and RV Park** in Hagensborg
Box 730, Bella Coola, BC, Canada V0T 1C0
Phone (250) 982-2504

# Highway Distances to the Bella Coola River

**From:**

- Vancouver, BC - 990 km. (614 miles)
- Blaine, WA, USA - border 980 km (608 miles)
- Calgary, AB - 1365 km. (847 miles)
- Edmonton, AB - 1450 km. (900 miles)

**Alternate Route**

As an alternate route to Bella Coola, BC Ferries operates a ferry from Port Hardy on Vancouver Island to Bella Coola. For information phone (250) 386-3431 or toll free in BC 1-888-223-3779.

## Atnarko River

Anglers visiting the Bella Coola River can fish another superb, famous and nearby waterway—the Atnarko River—with no effort whatsoever. You simply drive a few miles along the Bella Coola Valley, past Hagensborg, in the shadow of gigantic glaciers and rugged snow-topped mountains, until you are upstream of the confluence of the Talchako and Atnarko rivers. These two rivers join here to form the Bella Coola. You will know you're following the Atnarko, because the water is clear (except in freshet), unlike the Bella Coola and the Talchako, which are always turquoise-colored and a bit silted. Drive along the Atnarko and into the Fisheries Pool Campground where you will find plenty of good fish-holding water. This provincial park is rustic but quite convenient. Just remember that this particular area is famed for its large population of grizzly bears and black bears.

The same river-fishing guides recommended for the Bella Coola will guide you on the Atnarko.

**Vancouver Island**

# CHAPTER 9

# The Fabulous Fishy Cowichan

*A fly fisher is a man standing in cold water up to his liver, throwing the world's most expensive clothesline at trees.*

— P. J. O'ROURKE

Let's begin our visit to southeastern Vancouver Island's deservedly famous Cowichan River at an accessible spot on this great stream—Cowichan River Provincial Park, where there are two inexpensive, rustic campgrounds and plenty of pools that hold fish. Access to almost the entire river is easy on good roads and along the famed Cowichan Fishing Footpath.

From the city of Duncan, drive north on the Trans-Canada Highway, (Hwy 18). Turn left again on Riverbottom Road, which will take you first to Stoltz Pool Campground, then to Skutz Falls Campground. Each of these riverside Provincial Government campgrounds is located within walking distance of excellent fish-holding pools.

The clear, oxygen-rich waters of the lovely Cowichan River support large populations of brown trout, rainbow trout, cutthroat trout, chinook salmon, chum salmon and coho salmon during their spawning migrations. The river is also the home of steelhead and some Dolly Varden char.

## Brown Trout
Roderick Haig-Brown said the brown trout is "the finest trout, from a fly fisherman's point of view." In the Cowichan River, the brown

Cowichan River in Skutz Falls Campground.

trout is a sport fish of major importance. A European trout, the brown is not native to North America but was first introduced to this continent from Loch Leven in Scotland. The original plantings of brown trout in the Cowichan were made way back in the early 1930s.

After the initial plantings, browns were observed spawning in the Cowichan River in 1937, and they have long since become firmly established throughout the entire river system. In the Cowichan, immature browns feed primarily on stonefly nymphs, May fly nymphs and caddis larvae. Larger brown trout also eat insects but, in addition, they prey on crayfish, young salmon and other small fry. I know that Cowichan brown trout reach weights of five and six pounds, but I have heard rumors of some that weighed two or three times that much.

As with other trout, variations in color occur but, generally speaking, the brown trout is golden brown, with large black or dark brown spots, sometimes edged with orange. The spots below the lateral line and on the adipose fin are red or pink. The brown is a more consistent surface feeder than any of the other species of trout. It cruises and hovers just under the surface of the water, rather than lurking close to the bottom as do other trout species. Its willingness to feed at the surface is what makes the brown trout an ideal quarry for the dry fly fisher, but the brown is seldom an easy fish to catch. Because of a natural wariness, the brown trout is able to take care of itself very nicely.

The browns in the Cowichan have adapted well to their environment and are sustaining themselves with natural spawning, augmented by hatchery planting and intelligent regulations and restrictions—lately, there are indications that the brown trout population is increasing. Fishing is often best in the waters between Cowichan Lake and Skutz Falls, but there are several restrictions and closures on this part of the stream. Anglers really must study the British Columbia nontidal regulations very carefully before starting to fish.

Built by BC Forest Products in 1956, a low dam at Lake Cowichan Village—headwaters of the river—usually does a good job of controlling the flow of river water. Therefore, the upper Cowichan River can support healthy populations of resident trout, because the stream bottom is seldom scoured by flooding.

The virtual absence of flooding allows plankton and insects to thrive on nutrients derived, directly or indirectly, from the decaying carcasses of salmon that have died after spawning. The resulting abundance of insect life is what makes the upper Cowichan an outstanding fly fishing stream. However, there have been occasions when the water downstream has become too shallow for small fishing boats, and the flow at the dam hasn't always been increased to correct the situation.

In addition to the renowned Cowichan brown trout, there are populations of resident rainbow and cutthroat trout in the river.

From mid-October to late December, when salmon are spawning in the upper river, rainbow trout and browns lie in wait behind the salmon, grabbing loose eggs as they drift down to them in the current. This is a good time of year to fish for big trout, using egg-pattern flies.

## Rainbow and Cutthroat Trout

There are three seemingly different strains of rainbow trout in the upper Cowichan River—the first type being resident rainbows, often seven- to fourteen-inches in length. The second kind consists of lake rainbows that drop down in the winter to spawn in the spring. These fish usually are twelve- to eighteen-inchers. The third kind of "rainbows" actually are steelhead smolts, usually averaging about eight or nine inches in length.

Cowichan Lake, from which the fishy Cowichan River flows, is the second largest lake on Vancouver Island. This magnificent body of water has a provincial government campground, a municipal campground and a marina. Anglers nail some fine two- to six-pound cutthroat trout here, in addition to rainbows, kokanee and Dolly Varden char. Lake Cowichan village is situated at the lower end of the lake.

## Steelhead

Successful hatchery stocking and, perhaps, a smattering of good luck, have made the Cowichan River one of the finest winter steelhead streams on Vancouver Island. In 1997 when BC Fish and Wildlife discovered that the steelhead stocks were critically low in nine famous east coast Island rivers, the Cowichan's winter run remained in good shape.

To many anglers, the most exciting sport on the river is the winter steelheading, a highly specialized—and often chilling—form of river fishing. In the winter months near the Island Highway Bridge, or far upstream along the famed Fishing Footpath, the steelheader in waders and foul-weather clothing lives in optimistic anticipation that the next cast will result in a solid take by a tackle-straining fish.

Steelhead fishing on the Cowichan can be productive from December to April, but you can't always count on it. There have been winters when fishing was poor until a sizeable run arrived in January, followed by a slowdown in action until more steelhead moved into the river in large numbers in March. Following the footpath upstream from Holt Creek, visiting anglers can easily locate the well-beaten trails leading to the river and the most popular steelhead pools and runs. Most Cowichan steelhead weigh between six and eleven pounds, but occasionally a steelheader nails a twenty-pounder.

A visiting angler may fish this river for steelhead and have some success without a fishing guide. However, a local professional guide—like Dave Gunn of River Quest Charters—can be a tremendous help in teaching the most productive techniques, and in showing the visiting fishermen the locations of the best pools and runs. You'll find Dave's River Quest Charters listed in the "Where is What" section following this chapter.

Catching steelhead, even on bait, is still a major challenge for some of us old unsophisticated fishermen, but there are many anglers nowadays who insist upon fishing for the big sea-going rainbows with flies exclusively. Admittedly, hooking a summer-run steelhead with fly tackle is not an unusual feat, but trying to coax a big, lethargic winter

*Above:* Guide David Gunn
is holding steelhead.
*Photo: River Quest Charters*

*Right:* Releasing steelhead
on the Cowichan River.
*Photo: River Quest Charters*

steelhead in icy water to move even a few inches from his comfortable resting place to chase a fly has to be one of the toughest challenges in sport fishing.

There are steelhead fly fishermen who tell me that the selection of proper fly patterns is crucial; other fly casters insist that patterns are a minor consideration, but presentation is the key factor for success. Be that as it may, there is no question that certain fly patterns are very attractive to anglers, if not to the fish. Just ask a salesperson in a tackle shop.

## Cowichan Coho Salmon

The Cowichan coho salmon run usually peaks in late October, dependent on weather, water height, water temperature and other variables known only to the fish. One morning during a recent coho run, when my wife and I were camping at Skutz Falls, I wandered downstream past the wood bridge towards the Horseshoe Bend Pools. In one short stretch I met a surprisingly large number of coho fishing aficionados, mostly residents of Victoria, Duncan, Parksville or Nanaimo—and all veteran Cowichan anglers. It seems to me the easily-accessible, attractive Cowichan River—with its coho and chinook salmon, steelhead, brown trout, cutthroat and resident rainbow trout—attracts more southern Vancouver Island angling enthusiasts than does any other stream.

Coho salmon have been known to show an interest in a wide variety of baits, lures, wet flies and streamer flies. At certain times when the coho are moving upriver, they can be taken on just about any lure you throw at them, but only when the coho themselves wish to strike. These fish will sometimes refuse to bite for days on end, and there seems to be nothing an angler can do about it. However, even when the large coho won't cooperate, the small jack coho can frequently be coaxed into chasing some sort of lure, fly or bait.

In the autumn, when the coho salmon are milling around the ocean beaches near the mouth of the Cowichan River, waiting for a couple of rainy days to bring the river up to an acceptable level, some knowledgeable beach-casters and anglers in belly-boats enjoy exciting fly fishing. Mickey Finn, Chartreuse Popsicle and Coho Sunset are suitable fly patterns. But remember this: the waters inside Cowichan Bay (at the lower end of the river) are closed to fishing in August, September and October.

The Cowichan River

# Chinook Salmon

The Cowichan River supports a good September-October run of chinook salmon, and fishing regulations allow anglers to keep four chinooks under twenty inches long. The stream's chinook salmon receive a great deal of help from the Cowichan Indian Band members who own and operate a highly successful salmon hatchery on the river. Their facility has a rearing capacity of over three million chinook smolts annually.

Duncan, the City of Totems, is situated on the lower end of the Cowichan River. In the downtown area and along the approaches to the town there are twenty-two magnificent totem poles, each one a legitimate work of art, carved from old-growth cedar trees by Cowichan artisans. These totems represent sacred spirits, family histories, tribal rituals and ancient legends. Much of the land surrounding the city of Duncan and along the Cowichan River Valley belongs to the Cowichan Band, the largest band in British Columbia. Cowichan Indian sweaters are great for winter fishing. You can buy the original, genuine, warm Cowichan Indian sweaters at Quw'utsum' Cultural Center and Gift Shop at 200 Cowichan Way in Duncan.

Below the city of Duncan the river slides into the sheltered waters of Cowichan Bay. The picturesque little village of Cowichan Bay rests serenely in a protected cove, in a salty marine setting with old wood-frame houses perched on pilings over the water, houseboats and small craft moored at tiny wharves, walkways and short piers. Salmon and crab boats tie up at the commercial dock, and trailered sport fishing boats are launched at the community's fine boat ramp.

# The Famous Cowichan Fishing Footpath

In the 1950s the Cowichan Fish and Game Association members felt that the day was fast approaching when most public access to the Cowichan River would be lost. In the 1960s the rod-and-gunners constructed a footpath through the thick bush along the river, from their club property near the city of Duncan, to Skutz Falls.

Heading upriver on the footpath, hikers and anglers and other nature lovers see a great variety of plants, including enormous sword ferns, salal, thistles, edible mushrooms and even pink fawn lilies and wild ginger. The trail leads past some popular fishing holes and, after a couple of miles, the forest path leaves the river momentarily to return to the water at a spot frequented by great bald eagles in late fall and early winter. The trail winds through heavily treed woodlands to two grassy picnic areas, thence to Marie Canyon, Mayo Creek, the Horseshoe Bend Pools and the wooden bridge over the Cowichan at Skutz Falls Campground.

Perhaps Joe Saysell is the Cowichan River's best friend.

Fishing guide Saysell spent his childhood in a house on the marge of the river where he landed his first steelhead at the ripe old age of eight, when he was already a veteran angler with two years' experience fishing the stream. Joe's present home is also on the shore of the Cowichan.

For over forty years, Joe Saysell pleaded and battled to save the Cowichan River from urbanization, unwise logging practices and other dangers. As an active member of the BC Wildlife Federation, the Steelhead Society and the Valley Fish and Game Club, he continually championed his beloved river, its wild natural beauty, its fish and wildlife and their habitat. In 1992, he was awarded both the Totem Flyfishers' Roderick Haig-Brown Conservation Award and the Steelhead Society's Cal Woods Conservation Award.

The Cowichan River received special status in the BC Heritage Rivers Program in 1996, when the provincial government purchased private lands for a protective park corridor along the river. Joe Saysell was elated! The fact that the Cowichan is the most fish-rich stream on the east side of Vancouver Island is due, in part, to Joe's ceaseless efforts.

The Cowichan truly is a remarkable river. Even today, with fishing closures throughout British Columbia, an angler on the Cowichan can fish for and keep a few salmon, trout or steelhead. But anglers absolutely must study the current fishing regulations with extreme care, because there are a helluva lot of restrictions on this great river—and changes in the regulations can occur at any moment.

## Gamefish Species

Steelhead, resident brown trout, rainbow trout, cutthroat trout, Dolly Varden char, chinook salmon, chum salmon, coho salmon. An angler may fish in one part or another of the Cowichan River for one species of gamefish or another, but regulations, openings, closings and many restrictions can be confusing if the angler doesn't sit down for several days with his lawyer to interpret the provincial regulations.

## Fishing Regulations and Restrictions

- Single barbless hook.

- Bait ban, but there are exceptions: Bait may be used above Stanley Creek from April 16 to Nov. 14, and below Highway 1 Bridge in Duncan year-round. Fly fishing only from signs at Stanley Creek to CNR Bridge (mile 70.2).

- Boat speed restriction: 8 km/hr. Boat motor restriction 10 hp in some places. No fishing from dam at Cowichan Lake outlet to Stanley Creek, Nov. 15 to April 15.

- No fishing in Holt Creek and tributaries of the Cowichan River above Holt Creek.

- No fishing from CNR trestle at Mile 66 to 50 meters below the confluence with the unnamed creek that drains Mayo Lake, from Oct. 10 to Dec. 15.

- No fishing from boundary signs above town of Duncan pumphouse to Allenby Road Bridge from Sept. 1 to Dec. 15.

- Wild and hatchery trout and char over 30 cm, daily quota is 2 above trestle at Greendale Road in Lake Cowichan Village.

- Wild trout and char release from trestle at Greendale Road in Lake Cowichan to Skutz Falls.

- Hatchery trout and char over 30 cm, daily quota — 2 from Stanley Creek to CNR Bridge at Mile 70.2.

- Cutthroat trout and wild brown trout release below Skutz Falls.

- Steelhead: daily catch limit - 2 hatchery steelhead. Release all wild steelhead.
- Chinook salmon: quota — 4 per day. Release all over 50 cm in length.
- Coho salmon: quota — 1 per day. Release all over 35 cm.
- Chum salmon: closed to fishing.

For more info on regulations, including new closures:
- www.bcfisheries.gov.bc.ca
- Phone (250) 751-3100, (250) 746-1236, (250) 746-6221

## Lures & Flies

Because there are so many species of fish in the great Cowichan River and because fishing is open somewhere along the stream in every month of the year, for some species of gamefish, one could honestly say that any salmon or trout lure could catch a fish somewhere in the Cowichan River at some time or other.

- **Wet Flies for Trout and Char:** Pheasant Tail Nymphs, Muddler Minnow, Egg'n'Eye, Mohair Caddis Larva, Coachman, Royal Coachman, Stonefly Nymphs, Mayfly Nymph.
- **Dry Flies:** Tom Thumb, Deer Hair Caddis. Mosquito, Humpy, Lady McConnell, and anything you have in your fly box.
- **Lures for Trout and Char:** Small to medium-size weighted spinners and any of the myriad of wobbling spoons and Flatfish-type plugs.
- **Lures for Steelhead:** Wobbling spoons, particularly chrome-colored, Drift lures, Plastic fluorescent imitation worms, fluorescent yarn.
- **Steelhead Flies:** Black Practitioner, Squamish Poacher, Umpqua Special, Skykomish Sunrise, Skunk, Cowichan Special.
- **Chinook Salmon Lures:** Wiggle Wart plugs, Hottentot plugs, Kitimat spoons, Koho spoons, Spin'n'Glo drift lures.
- **Coho Lures:** Small and medium-size Krocodile spoons, Koho spoons, small size Wiggle Wart plugs. Small to medium-size Kitimat spoons.
- **Coho Flies:** Coho Sunset, Clouser, Mickey Finn, Chartreuse Popsicle.

# Guides, Outfitters, Charters, River Tours

**Dave Gunn, River Quest Charters**
5650 W. Riverbottom Road, Duncan, BC, V9L 6H9
Phone (250) 748-4776, (250) 748-4769

Guide Dave has been fishing the Cowichan for decades, and he knows how to find the fish for you. Dave offers you the ultimate winter steelhead experience. Bring your own boat or enjoy a professionally guided trip in River Quest's safe 16-foot welded aluminum drift boats, with licenced and insured guides. Cabins available.

**Jim Macovichuk**
River-fishing guide at Summer-Place-on-the-River
5245 Winchester Road, Duncan, BC V9L 1N9
Phone (250) 715-1222

Cowichan River steelhead.  *Photo: River Quest Charters*

# Tackle Shops

**Bucky's Sport Shop**
171 Craig Street, Duncan, BC, V9L 1B8
Phone (250) 746-4923

**Outdoor Explorers in Duncan**
Phone (250) 715-0900

# Visitor Info

**Cowichan River Visitor Information**
Phone (250) 715-0709
Toll free 1-888-303-3337
Fax (250) 715-0710
Email tourism@cowichan.com

**Lake Cowichan Village Visitor Information**
Phone (250) 749-3244, Fax (250) 749-0187
Email: chamber@clias.org

**Duncan & Cowichan Bay Visitor Center**
Phone (250) 746-4636, Fax (250) 746-8222
Email duncancc@islandnet.com
Website www.duncancc.bc.ca

# Accommodations

**Cowichan River Provincial Park**
Stoltz River Campground and Skutz Falls Campground
For information contact:

**BC Parks South Vancouver Island District**
2930 Trans Canada Highway, Victoria, BC, Canada V9E 1K3
Phone (250) 391-2300, Fax (250) 478-9211

**Duncan RV Park and Campground** on Cowichan River
2950 Boys Road, Duncan, BC, Canada V9L 6W4

**Riverside Campground**
1-3065 Allenby Road, Duncan, BC, Canada V9L 6W5

**Duncan Motel**
2552 Alexander Street, Duncan, BC, Canada V9L 2W9

**Best Western Cowichan Valley Inn**
6474 Trans Canada Highway
Phone (250) 748-2722
Fax: (250) 748-2207
Toll Free: 1-800-927-6199
Email: bwcvi@island.net
Website: www.bestwestern.com

**Summer Place Inn on the River**
5245 Winchester Road,
Phone: (250) 715-1222
Fax: (250) 746-0610
Email: info@summerplaceinn.com
Website: www.summerplaceinn.com *or*
www.summerplacelodge.com
Only steps away from great fishing on the Cowichan River.

**Travelodge Silver Bridge Inn**
140 Trans Canada Highway
Phone (250) 748-4311
Fax (250) 748-1774
Toll Free: 1-888-858-2200
Email: silverbridge@home.com

**Village Green Inn**
141 Trans Canada Highway
Tel/Fax (250) 746 5126
Toll Free: 1-800-655-3989
Email: villagegreen@bctravel.com

**Sahtlam Lodge & Cabins**
5720 Riverbottom Road West
Phone 1-877-748-7738
Email: cabins@sahtlamlodge.com

# Distances to the Cowichan River
**From:**

- Vancouver, BC — 75 km. (46 miles)
- Blaine, WA, USA border — 72 km. (45 miles)
- Calgary, AB — 1030 km (639 miles)
- Edmonton, AB — 1220 km (758 miles)

(Distances shown do not include the ferry trip from the mainland to Vancouver Island)

# BC Ferries Information
**From Mainland BC to Vancouver Island**

- Phone 1-888-223-3779 toll free from anywhere in BC
- Fax (250) 381-5452 for reservations
- Vancouver Island routes: phone 1-888-724-5223 toll free in BC. / (604) 444-2890 if you call from outside BC.
- For ferry travel information on the Internet: www.bcferries.com

Although the Cowichan River is an incredibly great angling stream, some sportfishers may wish to sample the fishing in other nearby waters. Some worthwhile suggestions would be Cowichan Lake, Nanaimo River, Little Qualicum River and Big Qualicum River.

# CHAPTER 10

## Gold Riverdancers

*We had a glass of beer and I admired Karl Dushenka's steelhead
—a beautiful thing, solidly silver and streamlined as a missile.
"What kind of lure did you use?"
"A hook."
"Where did you catch it?"
"In the water."*

— BERT DONOVAN
Editor, *Gold River Record* 1970

The Gold River on the west coast of Vancouver Island is the fifth most productive steelhead stream in the province of British Columbia. The Gold has excellent runs of summer steelhead. The month of June is a good bet for these exceptional gamefish, but you're liable to encounter them any time between April and September. Summer-run steelhead usually are much more active than the winter-run variety. Although the Gold River's winter steelhead are magnificent battlers, they tend to rest deep in their preferred holding pools, and seldom do they swim very far through chilly wintry water to grab a bait fish, an artificial fly or a lure.

The summer-run fish are different. In the warmer water they will chase a fly or lure halfway across the stream, smack it with gusto, then explode straight up into the stratosphere in spectacular leaps. The summer steelhead can teach you how to dance on water. These silvery, streamlined, rocket-propelled fish truly are riverdancers.

One veteran angler who knew plenty about the Gold River's steelhead and its salmon, trout, birds and animal, was long-time Gold

River resident Karl Dushenka. Probably the most successful—and undoubtedly the most notorious—fisherman ever to wade these lovely waters was the late Karl Dushenka.

You may hear hundreds of wild fish stories about Karl, but here's one that's become a major item in this community's local folklore. In the 1970s, when Governor-General Roland Michener visited Gold River, hotel chef Moe Adams was preparing a lavish banquet for the visiting dignitary and his entourage. Dinner was scheduled for seven p.m., but at one o'clock in the afternoon Moe, who planned to prepare a seafood side dish for this important occasion, suddenly realized he had no fresh fish.

Looking around the hotel beer parlor, Moe spotted Karl Dushenka and told him of his predicament. "I need a fish now! Please see what you can do for me!"

Karl gulped down his beer, grabbed his fishing rod and headed for the river. He returned in less than two hours with a steelhead that chef Adams describes as "the brightest and most perfect steelhead I ever saw."

In the el Niño warm years of the late 1990s, these warmwater fish were found swimming near the river mouth.

Derryl Calen and steelhead.

*Photo: Vaughn Michaud*

Our famed West Coast Island steelhead stream, the Gold River flows out of Gold Lake, nestled in splendid alpine wilderness in the extreme northwest corner of Strathcona Park. Heading westward the young mountain stream gathers in the waters of tiny Twaddle Lake and Waring Creek, then makes a sharp left turn and surges southward to the mouth of the Muchalat River. Upstream of this confluence the Gold River is completely closed to angling for all species of fish. This closure doesn't apply to lakes in the area.

A road westward from here leads to a wilderness campground at Muchalat Lake, with its thirty-seven campsites, picnic tables and a seaplane dock. This lake has fairly large populations of Dolly Varden char, kokanee, cutthroat trout and rainbow trout.

Campers, anglers and other nature lovers in the Gold River Valley are likely to get a glimpse of eagles, hawks, jays, deer, elk, black bears, mink, otters, cougars or beavers. Most river fishers can tell a few good bear stories, but here is something different—a really unusual Beaver story: In 1969, Gold River's most renowned angler, Karl Dushenka, hooked into what he believed was a world record chinook salmon. However, when he reeled it in close to shore, after a long, tough battle, he was shocked to discover it was a fair-sized beaver! Karl gently unhooked the animal and, when last seen, the catch-and-release beaver was happily swimming away—as far away as possible from the surprised fisherman.

South of the mouth of the Muchalat River the famous, fishy Gold River flows through the village that bears its name—the community of Gold River. This surprisingly neat, well-planned village has a woodsy public area known as Peppercorn Park on the banks of the Gold River. The park has a rough hiking trail through a veritable rain forest with ferns, mosses, dense underbrush, cedars, alders, huckleberries, salmonberries and various wildflowers. Strolling along the trail on the bank of the river, visitors will see some good fish-holding pools and several natural swimming holes. Peppercorn Park is a nature lover's haven.

In addition to the Gold River itself, there are other good angling waters nearby. Antler Lake and Upana Lake both offer fly fishing for trout (up to twelve inches). The most important tributary of the Gold, the Heber River, joins its mother stream at the southern end of town. The little Heber is a popular catch-and-release summer steelhead river—particularly between May and September.

There is access into much of this famous steelhead stream by roads and trails, but first-time visitors will benefit tremendously by considering a professional fishing guide on their first couple of forays into the Gold River valley. See the "What's Where" section at the end of this narrative for recommended guides.

On the splendid Gold River, south of the townsite, is the Lions Club Campsite, located on the west bank of the big stream. It's rustic, unpretentious and inexpensive. Here is how my wife Pauline describes the riverside campground: "This is my idea of a perfect place for a peaceful night's rest, with the quiet song of the babbling river slipping by, just a few yards from my pillow."

On one of our Gold River safaris, we drove our camper into the Lions Campground in the evening and parked close to the river. Next day, I picked up a camera and hiked upstream and down,

Gordon Davies and spinning rod on the "Big Bend" loop, Gold River.

searching for some worthwhile photos. About mid-afternoon I returned to our campsite, put my camera away, then proceeded to guzzle a cup of coffee.

Suddenly I heard the muffled but unmistakable sound of a screaming fishing reel. A faint, distant voice yelled, "I've got a fish on! It's a big one!" I rushed outside and began looking everywhere along the river for an angler who had hooked a big fish. I investigated every likely spot along the riverbank, but to no avail. I didn't see anyone anywhere.

Finally I gave up the search, but I seriously contemplated the possibility that my mind was out of synch, or perhaps we were camping in the Twilight Zone.

In the afternoon of the next day I was in the camper when, incredibly I heard a screaming reel and a muffled voice shouting excitedly,

"I've got a fish on! It's a big one!" This time I didn't run outside to look for the phantom fisherman. I traced the sound to its source. It seemed to be emanating from a top cupboard in the camper, which made no sense at all to me. However, I began emptying the cupboard until I came to a wrapped parcel that I didn't recognize. Eureka! In the parcel was the answer to the inexplicable sounds—a box with the name "Screamin' Reel" printed on the box top.

And then I remembered!

Shortly before we pulled into the Lions Campground we had purchased a birthday gift for one of our sons—we bought him one of the fabulous, unique "Screamin' Reel" Alarm Clocks. These unusual timepieces are authentic replicas of the large, reliable, popular Peetz hardwood-and-brass salmon reels with very handsome, reliable alarm clocks built into one side. The store clerk who demonstrated the reel-clock to us had obviously failed to shut off the alarm before she wrapped the clock. On these clocks, the alarm is not a bell or buzzer. The alarm is a screaming reel sound, together with a voice yelling, "I've got a fish on!"

So the alarm went off, right on time, two afternoons in a row, before I realized what was happening. Because the clock was wrapped and stored in a cupboard, the sounds were muffled, creating the impression that they were emanating from a short distance away, outside our camper.

## Summer-run Steelhead — the Riverdancers

The high-jumping, tail-walking, rocket-propelled, summer-run steelhead are the riverdancers of the Gold River. Much of the fishing for summer-runs takes place downstream from the Lions Campground and halfway to the river mouth at Muchalat Inlet. Along this stretch, the great Gold River flows along the bottom of deep, steep canyons, where steelhead anglers will find rapids, a waterfall, dangerous fast-water obstacles and a bit of difficult access—but they could also encounter some lovely, hard-fighting steelhead. First-time visitors to the Gold River would be well advised to hire professional fishing guides. There are several in town. Not only will anglers learn the location of good holding water for steelhead, but their chances of hooking fish will also be much greater if they have the help of local guides.

Nowadays all steelhead angling in the Gold River (and its tributary, the Heber) is catch-and-release. These steelhead are all wild fish. No hatchery steelhead are planted here! Summer-runs migrate up the river in spring and summer. May to August is normally a good bet. Pleasant weather and summery water temperatures make for exciting sport with the Gold River's summer steelhead.

Quite possibly, Gold River steelhead have been hooked on every artificial fly known to mortal man but you will find a few favorite steelhead patterns in the "WHAT'S WHERE?" section at the end of this chapter.

In June, 1998, at the Lions Club Campground local angler Jack Swan told me he had recently seen some anglers on the river behind the golf course clubhouse, where they were hooking and releasing quite a few steelhead. Pauline and I checked this out next morning but, when we arrived, there were no fishermen and no fish. As most sportfishers know, it is just this kind of scenario that spawned the familiar angling expression, "You should have been here yesterday."

## Winter-Run Steelhead

Someone once described winter steelheading as "hours and hours of monotonous casting spiced with a few minutes of nerve-shattering excitement." If you don't believe this definition—and you've never fished for steelhead in January—just try it! But be sure you wear long thermal underwear, heavy wool socks, Indian sweater, Balaclava hood, parka, gloves and insulated chest waders.

Winter fish can usually be found in the Gold River between January and March. Often the peak of the run arrives in February, with many fish being taken near the community of Gold River or in the popular Helicopter Run at the lower end of the stream. There are no monster-size forty-pound giant steelhead in the Gold River system. Any fish that weighs a little bit less than 20 pounds is a biggie here. Six-to ten-pounders are common.

The splendid Gold River—surprisingly deep in many spots—has spawning runs of sea-going cutthroat trout and Dolly Varden char, and a small resident population of fat, sassy, silvery rainbow trout. This first-rate waterway also hosts some salmon runs, including big, heavy, hard-fighting chinooks.

And now, just a mention of the fine saltchuck fishing available off the mouth of the Gold River. In Gold River village you can find reliable saltwater fishing charters that will take you to excellent fishing grounds in Muchalat Inlet and Nootka Sound for hot and heavy action with salmon, halibut to 200 pounds, lingcod, red snapper and a variety of other tasty bottomfish. Some guiding outfits like Vaughn Michaud's Nootka Sound Sportfishing will guide you on the saltwater and also on the river.

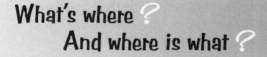

## What's where ?
## And where is what ?

## Gamefish Species
Steelhead, rainbow trout, cutthroat trout, Dolly Varden char, salmon.

## Restrictions
- Single barbless hook and bait ban.
- Release all trout and char less than 30 centimeters in length.
- Release ALL cutthroat trout.
- Release ALL steelhead. All Gold River steelhead are wild fish. There are no hatchery steelhead in the Gold.
- Release all salmon.

For further information on angling regulations and restrictions, phone BC Fish & Wildlife (250) 286-7630. BC Fisheries website: www.bcfisheries.gov.bc.ca

## Angling Methods

### Fly fishing
Some popular steelhead flies: Deschutes Special, Steelhead Bee, Coquihalla Orange, Woolly Bugger, Tiger Prawn, Skykomish Sunrise, Black Practitioner, Home Run, Skunk, Egg-sucking Leech, Bucktail McGinty, General Practitioner, Squamish Poacher.

### Flies for Trout and Dollies

There are thousands of patterns of trout flies to choose from, but here are a few popular patterns that will do the job: Coachman, Royal Coachman, Black Gnat, Black Woolly Worm, March Brown, Mickey Finn, Muddler Minnow, Black Ant.

### Spinning

Wobblers, weighted spinners, plastic pink bubble gum worms, drift lures (e.g. Spin-n-Glo, Gooey Bob)

### Float Fishing

(Not to be confused with the Washington-Oregon sport of drifting downstream in a river boat.)

British Columbia float-fishing is a sport imported from Britain a hundred years ago. Simply put, this sport requires casting a cork or plastic float (bobber) with bait or an artificial lure. Much more than this abbreviated description is required in float-fishing, and the only easy way to master the technique is to get instruction from an experienced west coast BC practitioner of the sport. A rather lightweight eight-foot to twelve-foot rod is required.

## Seasons for Gold River

Best time for summer steelhead is May to August. Winter steelhead fishing can be good from January to March.

## Guides, Outfitters, Charters, River Tours

**Nootka Sound Sports Fishing Charters and Whale Watching**
Vaughn H. Michaud
P.O. Box 176, Gold River, BC, Canada V0P 1G0
Tel/fax: (250) 283-7194, Toll Free Phone 1-877-283-7194
email: nootka@island.net
www.nootkasoundfish.com

Accommodations, meals, equipment, beachcombing, kayaking, group rates.

Elaine and Vaughn Michaud holding two lovely Chinook Salmon from Nootka Sound off the mouth of the Gold River. *Photo: Nootka Sound Sport Fishing Charters*

Boss man Vaughn Michaud at Nootka Sound Charters says they spend most of their time guiding on the saltchuck in July and August. In the autumn, winter and spring they guide steelheaders on the Gold River, Heber River, Conuma River and Burman River.

**Top Guides Canada Inc.**
P.O. Box 20025, Campbell River, BC, Canada V9W 7Z5
Toll free 1-877-287-4475

**Maurice Graves**
Box 311, Gold River, BC, Canada V0P 1G0
Phone 250-283-2513

Maurice will guide anglers on the Gold River, even in the summer months, unlike other guides who concentrate on saltwater fishing in July and August. With his wife Dawne, Maurice operates the Shadowlands Bed and Breakfast.

# Tackle Shops

**The Tackle Box**
Ralph Osha, proprietor / phone (250) 283-2229
Open from May 15 to Labor Day at the Petrocan Service Station
on Muchalat Drive.

# Accommodations

**Lions Club Campground**
Rustic and inexpensive. On the Gold River, downstream from
Gold River village, past the Big Bend Road.

**Shadowlands Guest Lodge**
Maurice and Dawne Graves, proprietors
Box 311, Gold River, BC, Canada V0P 1G0
Phone (250) 283-2513

**Peppercorn Trail Motel**
Phone (250) 283-2443

**Ridgeview Motel**
Phone (800) 989-3393

For more information, phone Gold River Information Center
(250) 283-2418

# Highway Distances to the Gold River

**From:**
- Vancouver, BC — 240 km (143 miles)
- Blaine, WA USA border — 248 km (151 miles)
- Calgary, AB — 1215 km (754 miles)
- Edmonton, AB — 1395 km (866 miles)

(These distances do not include the ferry ride from the  mainland
to Vancouver Island.)

# BC Ferries Information

- Website: www.bcferries.com

## From Mainland BC to Vancouver Island

- Phone 1-888-223-3779 toll free from anywhere in BC
- Fax (250) 381-5452 for reservations.

## Vancouver Island routes

- phone 1-888-724-5223 toll free in BC
- or (604) 444-2890 if you call from outside BC

To drive to the Gold River from Campbell River City on the east coast of the Island, one must drive westward on Highway 29. While in Campbell River's downtown area, anglers should visit the world-famous Tyee Pool at the rivermouth, the great river's famed salmon and steelhead pools, the well-preserved Haig-Brown Home on the river shore, and the Campbell's famed tributary, the Quinsam River which, in autumn, produces some great catches of coho salmon.

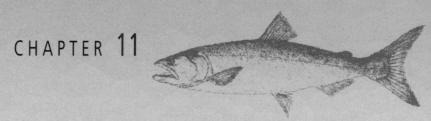

# CHAPTER 11

# North Island's Magnificent Marble River

plus the Quatse, Cluxewe and Nimpkish Rivers

*In wilderness is the preservation of the world*

— ELLIOT PORTER,. Sierra Club

I first learned of the remote, fishy Marble River from fly fisherman and river-lover Ken Thompson of Port Hardy at the north end of Vancouver Island. Ken, an expert fly-caster, described this marvelous stream, its steelhead and its resident trout, and I knew immediately that I must visit this exceptional waterway. I did—several times—and the Marble River proved to be even more magnificent than Ken said it was. For an accessible trout and steelhead stream, this is an incredibly natural and unspoiled river!

The incomparable Marble River has a few aliases. At its headwaters above Victoria Lake, the infant stream carries the name "Marble River," but as it leaves Victoria Lake and flows into Alice Lake it is known as the "Link River." From the lower end of Alice Lake to the ocean, it is the Marble River, except to an ornery group of Islanders who claim it is the "Amazon River." In the not-so-distant past, the aboriginal people called the river the "Sadzade" (meaning Chinook Salmon River).

Now that I have removed any possible confusion regarding the river's name, let's look at the alpine headwaters of this remarkable watercourse.

Near the small mill town of Port Alice on the west coast of northern Vancouver Island, a logging road leads to a mountain stream, born

Marble River.

Photo: Fly Rod Outfitters

in the wild five-thousand-foot-high hills. The infant river winds its way northward a short distance, then empties into Victoria Lake. This diminutive creek is the headwaters of the Marble River. Although the Marble flows northward, three other rivers—the Ououkinsh, Kashuti and the Kauwinch—originate in the same area as the Marble, then flow southward.

A few miles east of Port Alice, the Marble River (locally called the Link River)—a lovely, middlin'-small stream—meanders, tumbles and flows gently as it wanders north from Victoria Lake to slide quietly into the south end of Alice Lake. Angling in the Link River is restricted to fly fishing only, catch-and-release. There is a primitive, treed campground at the mouth of the Link River, with rough, natural campsites, a picnic park, playground and sandy bathing beach. We

The Marble River.

Photo: Flyrod Outfitters

camped here one day in mid-summer with our friends Vic and Alice Hay, and we had the campground, beach and picnic grounds all to ourselves. At the camp's mini-office I met a local chap who told me he regularly catches a fair number of trout from his car-top boat on the lake in sight of the mouth of the Link (alias Marble) River. I put in an hour or so fishing this spot from shore with flies, but I couldn't pitch the fly out far enough to reach the most likely-looking water. I must admit I didn't get even one strike, but I have a hunch this place could be productive in the springtime, when Dolly Varden char should be hanging around waiting for the trout to enter the Link River on their spawning run. There is nothing Dollies like more than following trout

Fly caster near bridge on Port Alice Road.

to their spawning beds, then gorging themselves on all the eggs they can steal.

For boaters, Alice Lake offers some good trolling for fairly big rainbow and cutthroat trout and Dolly Varden char, particularly in the spring and autumn. There is a good concrete boat-launching ramp at the north end of Alice Lake, upstream from the highway bridge (not far from the Marble River Fish hatchery). Another possibility for lake trollers is the launching ramp at the campground halfway along the wild east shore of Alice Lake.

Even if you have never before visited Northern Vancouver Island, you will have no difficulty in finding some of the finest pools and fish holding runs on the Marble River. Drive north on Highway 19, past Campbell River to Port McNeil, then continue heading north and turn left on the Port Alice Highway before you reach Port Hardy. After you pass little Sara Lake on your left, you'll come to a fairly large concrete bridge over a splendid, medium-size stream. This is the magnificent Marble River. Cross the bridge and turn right immediately on a secondary road that will lead you past a large, grassy, riverside picnic area. Drive on, keeping to the right, and you will find a forested campground with views of the river from some of its thirty-three free campsites—and plenty of peace and quiet.

From the campground (operated by Western Forest Products Ltd.) a three-mile trail leads downstream to a waterfall, rapids, and a fish ladder, but there are places along this path where the trail doesn't run close to the shore of the river. In fact, it will occasionally be necessary—and well worthwhile—to tromp through the bush, uphill and down over deadfalls, to reach an attractive pool, a picturesque grove of trees, or a logjam in the stream for the purpose of sketching, painting, photographing, bird watching or fly casting or, perhaps, simply contemplating the river's splendid, natural, wild charm.

In the summer of 1999 I watched two young fly fishermen catch and release six fine cutthroat trout here while I was shooting pictures of them and of other fly casters. The water was extremely high for mid-summer, but it was crystal clear. I wasn't surprised to see the clear, clean water because the curator of the Port Hardy museum had told me that the Marble River has the purest water in the entire north end of Vancouver Island.

From the bridge on the Port Alice Road, and downstream for a quarter of a mile, there is some glorious trout water that will gladden the heart of any true river lover. The Marble has medium-slow, fairly deep stretches, interspersed with fastwater runs and big, slippery, fallen tree trunks jammed behind large boulders leading out to midstream from the riverbank. Sure-footed fly fishers use these wet, slippery, treacherous "bridges" to walk on (with extreme care) so they can get into optimum casting position in mid-river. I have watched these daredevil tightrope-walkers hooking and releasing a goodly number of trout in a very short time.

From this dramatically spectacular stretch of water, downstream through the campground area, and within easy walking distance below the campsites, there is plenty of ideal water for trout and steelhead. Pauline and I camped along this fishy stretch of the Marble River several times in the late 1990s. We found the water clean and surprisingly clear, but rather high and fast. A couple of times I debated with myself on the advisability of wading in this possibly dangerous water and risking a dunking in the swift current, as I have done frequently all of my life. Now that I am eighty years old, I have been noticing that wading in turbulent rivers and walking on slippery logs over deep pools isn't quite as easy as it was when I was a forty or fifty-year-old youngster. So I settled for shooting photos of younger, more daring fly casters.

This doesn't mean I'll ever stop fishing in rivers—heaven forbid—but, in future, I'll try to stick to the slower-moving, less hazardous streams when wading.

The Marble River Fish Hatchery is located at the lower end of Alice Lake where the Marble flows out of the big lake. I met two members of the hatchery staff here, Rene Hunt and Lorraine Landry, who obligingly gave me a brief tour of their fish-raising facility and answered all my questions about the hatchery, the river and its fish. The hatchery folk welcome visitors.

The Marble River is home to summer steelhead (August and September), winter steelhead (February–March), resident rainbow trout, cutthroat trout, Dolly Varden char, chinook salmon and coho salmon. During a period of low coho returns in many other rivers, the Marble River's coho run fared very well. In 1998, when a majority of fisheries experts predicted small returns of spawning cohos, the Marble River's coho salmon showed up in surprisingly large numbers.

While researching materials for this Marble River tale I was surprised to learn that nobody I interviewed knew why the stream was named "Marble." In fact, most folks told me emphatically that there was no marble in the entire Marble watershed. I asked at the Port Hardy Library; but learned nothing about the origin of the river's name. Then I visited William Reeve, the knowledgeable curator of the Port Hardy Museum. I queried him regarding the name "Marble River" and I mentioned that other local folks had told me there is no marble in the area.

"I think I can help," said Mr. Reeve, "but I can only give you an educated guess."

He then produced a map with some strange (to me) markings on it, and he pointed to some squiggles in various locations on the map.

Mr. Reeve explained, "These marks indicate that marble has been discovered in all of these places, including the bottom end of the Marble River where it runs into the salt water. River fishermen and hikers would seldom visit this isolated part of the river, but early European explorers in sailing ships would have sent men in small boats into the estuary of the stream and they would have seen outcroppings of plain white marble in boulders along the shore. Because this plain white variety has almost no commercial value, it is likely that nobody will ever try to take any out of there."

My spouse Pauline and I are dyed-in-the-wool, incurable river lovers. Like many other anglers, campers, birdwatchers, photographers, and artists, we hear—and respond to—the irresistible siren call of the great outdoors when we stand on the marge of a racing, sparkling stream like the Marble. I am certain that some of us anglers are river-worshippers, for when we wade a wild river or meander along its banks we know we walk with the Supreme Creator. A peace greater than peace of mind or peace of soul comes to us when we stand at the water's edge and surrender all of our senses to the mystical, enchanting spell of the living river.

## What's where ?
## And where is what ?

## Game Fish Species
Cutthrout trout, resident rainbow trout, steelhead, Dolly Varden char, coho salmon, and chinook salmon.

## Regulations and Restrictions
- Single barbless hook, bait ban.
- Steelhead: Hatchery steelhead / 2 per day, minimum length 50 cm. Wild steelhead / release.
- Trout / Dolly Varden char / 2 per day, minimum length 30 cm.
- Salmon: all salmon must be released.

For more clarification of fishing regulations:

- Phone (250) 751-3100 or (250) 949-2800
- Fisheries (BC) www.monday.com/fishing
- Fisheries (Federal): pskf@direct.ca

## Lures & Flies

- **Dry Flies for Trout:** Adams, Tom Thumb, Coachman, Royal Coachman, Humpy, Dry Mosquito.

- **Wet Flies for Trout:** Woolly Worm, Black Gnat, Green Sedge, Muddler Minnow, Egg'n'Eye, Pheasant Tail Nymph and all other common trout flies.

- **Steelhead Flies:** Skunk, Skykomish Sunrise, Squamish Poacher, Black Practitioner, Deschutes Special, Purple Peril, General Practitioner and thousands of other steelhead patterns.

## Fishing Guides and Outfitters

### Fly Rod Outfitters
Box 1647, Port McNeil, BC V0N 2R0
Phone (250) 956-2706

Rodney Vuorela of Fly Rod Outfitters in Port McNeill, BC loves the Marble River. Rodney will provide you with a knowledgeable fishing guide.

### Top Guides Canada Inc.
Box 2002, Campbell River, BC V9W 7Z5
Phone toll free 1-877-287-4475

## Tackle Shops

### Port Hardy Marine Hardware
Tackle, fishing licences
6465 Hardy Bay Road, Port Hardy
Box 336, Port Hardy, BC V0N 2P0
Bud Young, phone (250) 949-6461

**Timberline Sports**
in Port McNeill
Phone (250) 956-3544

**Shop Rite Marine**
in Port McNeill
Phone (250) 956-3385

**Jim's Hardy Sports**
in Port Hardy
Phone (250) 949-8382

# Accommodations

A **free campground on the Marble River** is maintained by
Western Forest Products Ltd. A road from the Alice Lake Highway
Bridge (over the Marble) leads to this campground-in-the-forest.

**Pioneer Inn**
on the outskirts of Port Hardy
4965 Byng Avenue, Port Hardy, BC
Phone (250) 949-7271

**Quatse River Campground**
8400 Byng Road
Box 1409, Port Hardy, BC
Phone (250) 949-2395

# Highway Distances to the Marble River

**From:**
- Vancouver, BC — 415 km (258 miles)
- Blaine, WA USA border — 435 km (270 miles)
- Calgary, AB — 1375 km (854 miles)
- Edmonton, AB — 1480 km (919 miles)

(These distances do not include the ferry ride to Vancouver Island.)

Fly fisher, Ken Thompson of Port Hardy, B.C., on the Quatse River.

# Three More Nearby Island Rivers

Here are three rivers an angler can visit en route to or returning from the Marble River. Each of these streams can offer exciting sport at certain times of the year.

## Quatse River at Port Hardy

Logging roads and public roads crisscross and follow the gentle little Quatse River as it meanders, splashes and tumbles along on its journey from the hills above Coal Harbor to Port Hardy and the saltchuck. In this river valley, nature lovers, artists and photographers may find inspiration in the stillness of the deep green forest,

A 22-pound winter-run steelhead from the Quatse river in 1996, caught by Gerry Lambert.

and may be rewarded with glimpses of eagles, deer, elk, black bear and the most misunderstood animals on Vancouver Island, cougars. An adult cougar can kill a six-hundred-pound moose and its remarkable predatory abilities have resulted in many misconceptions, particularly a mistaken belief that cougars regularly prey upon humans. Over the past century, in the entire province of British Columbia, only seven people were killed by cougars. In the same hundred years, bees killed an estimated three hundred persons.

Although there are cutthroat trout in the Quatse, this waterway is primarily a winter steelhead stream. In the office of the Quatse River Campground at Port Hardy, you can admire the handsome twenty-two-pound winter-run steelhead caught by Gerry Lambert of Port Hardy in the Quatse in 1996. A true hatchery product, this mounted fish was hatched, raised and tagged at the Quatse River Hatchery.

On the river above and below the campground and downstream to the mouth, the good holding pools are easy to find. Season after season the winter steelheaders have stomped and trampled very distinct paths into all the best fishing holes.

# Cluxewe River
(Five kilometers northwest of Port McNeill)

Traditionally a good winter steelhead stream, the Cluxewe continues to produce reasonable numbers of these fine gamefish. Although anglers must release all steelhead caught in most east coast Vancouver Island streams, a fisherman may retain one hatchery steelhead per day on the little Cluxewe River. January to March is a good bet for steelheading here.

Sea-run cutthroat trout and big Dolly Varden char feed around the mouth of the Cluxewe in March, April and May. Experienced local fly fishers, like Jim 'Gully' Gullett of Port McNeill, often fare quite well during this springtime fishery. If you are an experienced west coast angler with an understanding of estuary trout fishing, you will have no problems. Otherwise hire a good guide.

Coho and chinook salmon both spawn here, but the pink salmon is unquestionably the main attraction. In mid-August of even-numbered years, extremely large schools of pinks (aka humpbacks or humpies) move into the shallow waters along the beach before spawning time, where thousands are caught daily by wading fly fishers. Make no mistake about this! Fly fishing for silver-bright pink salmon here in even-numbered years can be wild, fast and exhilarating! Many limits of pink are caught by fly casters along the shore where thousands of fish swim back and forth for weeks, until they feel like entering

Ian Dadswell (on right) boated this 110-pound halibut in 40-foot-deep waters off the mouth of the Cluxewe River.

Gordon Davies on saltwater beach at Cluxewe beach.

the river. Experienced fly casters do not need a fishing guide for this fish fest.

In mid-August, 1998, Fred and Penny Patrick accompanied my wife Pauline and me on a pleasant four-day visit to the Cluxewe's beach for a spot of pink salmon fishing. The fish were there in astronomical numbers when we arrived, and still were jumping and cavorting enthusiastically along the length of the beach when we were leaving. We caught, released and lost dozens of these small (three- to five-pound) salmon—but we kept a couple for supper every day. The meat of the pink salmon is tasty if it is cleaned and refrigerated promptly and cooked properly. Freezing can destroy much of its delicate flavor, but smoked pink salmon is a taste treat.

Most of our fish were taken on Pink Eve and Hoochie pink salmon flies, tied by Jim Gullett of Port McNeill.

## Nimpkish River
(Five kilometers southeast of Port McNeill)

This is the river that prompted Roderick Haig-Brown to say, "Whenever I think of a western fishing river, one typical of the best things that western fishing can offer, I think of the Nimpkish; and I expect I always shall."

Along the Nimpkish River, upstream from the community of Woss, there is some good winter steelhead fishing above the Old Duncan Bridge and near the Roan Road cut-off. December through March is the best bet for these great gamefish. Local steelhead fly fishers may tell you the names of their favorite feathered steelhead attractors although, as most river anglers realize, almost all the steelhead flies known to mortal man may catch these fish at certain times—but only if you know how to fish for steelhead. In this same part of the upper Nimpkish, fishermen may encounter resident cutthroat trout that can reach sixteen to eighteen inches in length.

Canada's (perhaps North America's) foremost river-angling writer, Rod Haig-Brown was one of the first sport fishermen to explore the pools of the lower Nimpkish River (the seven miles between Nimpkish Lake and the sea). In January, 1929, while employed in logging camps on the north end of Vancouver Island, he began to study and fish for winter steelhead. This was where Rod first began to amass his knowledge of these exceptional gamefish, eventually qualifying him as one of the world's foremost experts on steelhead angling.

The Nimpkish River (somewhere between its source and its mouth, and in proper seasons) has populations of steelhead, cutthroat and rainbow trout, Dolly Varden char, and kokanee, coho, chinook, pink, chum and sockeye salmon. The early summer run of sockeye salmon is often followed into the river by sea-run cutthroat trout who plan to dine on salmon eggs. Before setting forth to pur-

Awesome rapids near the village of Woss on the Nimpkish River.

sue these cutthroat trout, anglers should study the current BC angling regulations for possible new restrictions and closures.

The Nimpkish watershed, with its tributary streams and lakes, is sizeable. This is the type of water where an experienced guide can be of assistance. Rodney Vuorela of Fly Rod Outfitters in Port McNeill will provide you with a guide for the Nimpkish, Cluxewe and Quatse rivers. Phone him at (250) 956-2706. His mailing address is: Box 1647, Port McNeill, BC, Canada V0N 2R0.

# CHAPTER 12

# Stamp River's Steelhead and Salmon

*Any fisherman who tells you he does not care much whether or not he catches fish is a hypocrite and a liar.*

— JOHN F. FENNELL, 1960

I n south-central Vancouver Island the Stamp River—British Columbia's third most productive steelhead stream—flows out of the east end of Great Central Lake. This majestic lake is a long, narrow, deep body of water that offers exciting autumn trout fishing, beginning early in September. Winds on Great Central Lake can accelerate suddenly to high velocity, creating life-threatening hazards for small boats.

At the remote west end of this magnificent lake, a steep trail leads hikers to the highest waterfall in Canada—Della Falls, with a drop of one thousand, four hundred and forty feet. The fact that the Stamp River drains a large lake ensures that the stream, throughout its entire length, will always have a sufficient volume of water, even during so-called "low water" periods. Access to good pools on the Stamp is fairly easy by road and trail.

The Stamp's upper reaches flow northward, then the great river makes a U-turn, heads southeast and collects the waters of the Ash River, another important salmon and steelhead stream. Below the confluence of the Ash and the Stamp rivers is Money's Pool, the best-known piece of water on the Stamp, named in honor of General Noel Ernest Money, a veteran of the Boer War and the First World War, and

34-inch Stamp River steelhead.

Vancouver Island's most famous and successful angler in the early years of the twentieth century.

The General lived at Qualicum Beach, the seaside village he founded, and he fished most of the east-coast Island streams, but his favorite was a west coast river, the Stamp. He spent so much time at the Stamp River that he had a room reserved permanently at the Somass Hotel in nearby Port Alberni. In the 1930s, when the British Columbia government made a silent black-and-white documentary film on British Columbia sport fishing, the General and his long split-cane fly rod were the stars of the steelheading sequences. The cameras caught all the action as big bright Stamp River steelhead continually attacked the General's flies, then exploded through the water's surface to perform aerial acrobatics for the movie-makers.

Today, at the outset of a new millennium, General Money's beloved Stamp River still offers exceptional chinook salmon fishing, tolerable coho sport fishing and both summer and winter steelheading which, at times, can be first-rate. This latter-day quality angling is due almost entirely to the phenomenal success of the Robertson Creek Fish Hatchery at the headwaters of the Stamp. This astounding hatchery has an annual production of about eight million chinook salmon smolts, one million coho smolts and two hundred thousand steelhead

*Above:* Stamp River near Stamp Falls.

*Right:* Big chinook salmon from Stamp River.

smolts. This is a large, busy, highly successful facility that does a professional job of rebuilding depleted steelhead and salmon stocks in the Stamp River.

Besides being a popular steelhead fishing ground, Money's Pool and the waters above and below it can be very productive for coho fishing enthusiasts between September and November. In October, the prime coho-fishing month, the waters at or near Money's Pool often hold many clean, bright, coho salmon. The moderate current speeds in this stretch of river are conducive to light-tackle angling. Anglers with casting rods or spinning rods frequently use eight-pound-test line for coho; some fly fishers find a number-seven-weight outfit quite adequate here.

Some river anglers enjoy good fly fishing in the waters above and below Money's Pool, because Money's demands longer casts than they feel comfortable with.

Stamp River fly fishermen prefer the months of August, September and October for summer-run steelhead, but these anglers often experience difficulty in locating the steelies because their favorite pools and runs are packed full of salmon heading upstream to spawn. This situation doesn't always prevent experienced steelheaders from connecting with the sea-run rainbows, because the summer-runs often hold in shallow water, away from the crowded masses of salmon in the deeper holes. Under these conditions, in spite of the proximity of the salmon, the steelhead have been known to strike readily—morning, evening or mid-day.

This salmon is almost as big as the fisherman.

Nowadays, every neophyte fly fisher can find countless books and magazine articles on the subject of steelhead fly fishing. A visit to a tackle shop or a glance in a fly-tyer's catalog will reveal dozens of proven fly patterns, or variations on patterns. But steelhead fly fishing hasn't always been a popular sport. There was a time, from 1900 to 1950, when you could have counted all the steelhead fly fishers in British Columbia on the fingers of one hand, and you would have had enough fingers left over to knot a fly onto your leader tippet.

Back in those early days, famed fishing writer Roderick Haig-Brown described General Noel Money as "the finest and most experienced steelhead fly fisherman in British Columbia." Interestingly, on the subject of steelhead flies, the General believed that shape and size were more important than the color of the fly. Having said that, he admitted that he thought the steelies would respond best to a red fly. He preferred to start fishing with a red pattern and then, if necessary, he would change to a darker fly. Some of the steelhead patterns originated by the General—the Prawn Fly, General Money's Fly and Dick's Fly—enjoyed local popularity among the few steelhead fly fishers on Vancouver Island from the 1920s to the 1940s.

The Stamp's early winter steelhead run often arrives late in November, and peaks in December. Incidentally, if you aren't a west coast angler you may not know that the steelhead is a gourmet's delight. Its rich flesh is particularly tasty when baked or barbecued.

The most-visited spot on the river is Stamp Falls Provincial Park, with its treed campsites along the riverside, clean outhouses and fresh drinking water. It's a lovely primitive campground, and every camping spot is literally within a stone's throw of some of the finest river-fishing on Vancouver Island. While camping in the park, Pauline and I were serenaded daily by the fastwater river's bubbling melodies and, at night, by the stream's soothing liquid lullaby. Truly, the General's beloved Stamp River is an enchanted stream. At the lower end of the campground there is a trail that leads to safe viewing sites where visitors can marvel at the salmon (sockeye in summer, chinook and coho in the fall) attempting to navigate the fish ladder and leap the falls.

Below Stamp Falls a footpath leads along a narrow, steep, deep-sided canyon where the sun's rays reach the water at the bottom of the chasm only at mid-day in the spring, summer and fall. In wintertime, the bottom of the canyon remains dark, damp and gloomy all day long.

Along the river, throughout the campground, there is plenty of fine fishing water—easily accessible and often not too crowded. Anglers here frequently see black bears nonchalantly fishing nearby. Deer, cougar and various smaller animals also frequent the Stamp River Valley. Along the river grow stately cedar trees, bushy maples and gray-green alder, with an abundance of huckleberries, wild roses, Scotch thistles, buttercups, bleeding hearts and various ferns. Close to the water's edge, many trees are festooned with a variety of hanging mosses. A large part of the Stamp River Valley actually qualifies as a true rain forest.

On a sunny day in early October, I was fishing for chinook salmon at the upper end of the campground and, for an hour, the only company I had was a black bear directly across the river from me. I would make several casts, and the bear would stop and study the water on his side of the stream. Then I moved along a few yards and started casting again, while the bear strolled casually along, stopped and gave the water another look. And so it went. Every time I moved, the bear moved.

Then, without warning, the routine changed. I walked along the riverbank a short distance, stopped and looked across the water, expecting to see my hairy fishing partner. But he was gone. He had sneaked off into the bush without so much as an "adios." And then it occurred to me: that old bear, the great wild hunter, hadn't caught a single fish! I don't think he even saw one. But then, I asked myself, who was I to criticize the noble animal? I hadn't caught anything either!

There are some delightful stretches of water at the upstream end of the campground, with good flat beaches to run on when you are chasing a hooked fish that decides to race downstream at full speed until it breaks your line. Some of the best pools and runs downriver have rapids above or below, and steep banks with patches of thick brush at the shoreline. These conditions can prevent an angler from maintaining any degree of control over a big salmon if it takes a notion to swim out of the pool.

Late September usually is a good time to visit the Stamp River for chinook fishing. Stamp chinooks average about twenty pounds in weight, and there are jack chinook that weigh less than seven pounds. At the other extreme, there are giants that tip the scales at over forty pounds! By the second week of October, almost all of these migrating chinooks have lost every trace of their saltchuck sheen, and many are charcoal-colored. In spite of this, a few of the chinook caught in the park pools in October are in surprisingly good condition. When Pauline and I were at the campground in October, 1991, I watched an angler landing a bright twenty-five-pounder and a very clean seven-pound jack while fishing right behind his parked vehicle.

A mile or so downstream from Stamp Falls is a pool about the size of Money's. The easiest way to reach this pool is to follow a long trail from the main road near the site of the old Stamp Falls General Store. The trail begins at a sizeable grove of large maple trees, and leads you down a long, very steep grade, known to some anglers as "Heart Attack Hill," to the big pool on the river.

Farther downriver, at the end of McKenzie Road, where the river is wide, powerful and magnificent, you'll find Galaxy Way Campground. Franz, the camp's boss man, tells campers and anglers they are welcome to use his "Fisherman's Trail" downriver along the marge of the great stream. Down this pathway one mile there are resident trout, sea-run fish and beaver dams. When the salmon migrate upstream in the autumn, the prolific maple trees here are a rich golden color, contrasting with the deep green of tall cedar trees. Below McKenzie Road, the Sproat River joins the Stamp. From the confluence of the Sproat and the Stamp, the stream flows on for several miles under the name "Somass River" until it spills into Alberni Inlet.

Today, gazing down upon his beloved Stamp River from the part of Heaven that the River Gods have reserved for fly fishermen, General Money cannot be totally disappointed at the condition of the great Island stream. The Stamp still runs wild and free through much of its length. Its salmon and steelhead runs, with help from the hatchery, are large.

And—even though the Stamp has its share of poachers and snaggers—the fly-fishing General must be pleased to see that most of today's anglers, young and old alike, are law-abiding, respectful, ethical sportsmen.

# What's where?
## And where is what?

## Gamefish Species

Chinook salmon, coho salmon, steelhead, some resident trout, some sea-run trout.

## Gear Restrictions

- Single barbless hook.
- Bait may be used only from November 1 to April 30 below signs at Girl Guide Falls (upstream from mouth of Beaver Creek).
- Bait ban all year above the signs at Girl Guide Falls.

## Regulations

- Boat motors restricted to 10 hp on some parts of the river.
- June 15 to November 15, closed to fishing from 200 meters above Stamp Falls to 500 meters below Stamp Falls.
- December 1 to April 30, closed to fishing from the confluence with Ash River upstream to Great Central Lake.
- Catch-and-release wild steelhead, cutthroat trout, Dolly Varden.

**Catch Limits on Salmon and Hatchery Steelhead**

These limits change from season to season (or moment to moment). For an update on current daily limits:

- www.bcfisheries.gov.bc.ca
- phone (250) 724-9290, (250) 724-0195, (250) 751-3100, (250) 756-7192 or call toll free to Salmon Regulations Update Line (877) 320-3467.

## Angling Methods

Fly fishing, spinning, stripcasting, or casting with level-wind reels.

Float-fishing with a float (bobber) and bait or artificial lure is a popular old method preferred by many successful, experienced west coast steelheaders. A 9-foot to 12-foot two-handed rod works well for this technique.

- **Coho Salmon Flies:** Cathy's Coat, Coho Blue, Coho Peacock, Yellow Peril
- **Steelhead Flies:** Squamish Poacher, General Practitioner, Black Practitioner, Davie Street Hooker, Skykomish Sunrise, Skunk, Deschutes Special, Umpqua Special and a million other patterns.
- **Steelhead and Salmon Lures:** Gibbs Koho Spoon, Gibbs Kitimat Spoon, Krocodile wobblers in various sizes, Five-of-Diamonds Spoons.
- **Bait When, Where and If Legal for Float Fishing:** Float fishing ("float" is a BC, and British, word for "bobber") ghost shrimp, dew worms (nightcrawlers), salmon roe. **Artificials for float fishing:** Spin'n'Glo, Cherry Bobber. Long, fluorescent plastic worms (red, orange or pink).

## River Tours, Outfitters, Guides

**Bob Welsh, West Coast Outfitting**
Box 1219, Port Alberni, BC, V9Y 7M1
Phone (250) 723-1009

**Castaway Guide Service**
Phone (250) 720-7889

**Murphy's Sportfishing**
Phone (250) 723-2772

**Ogilvie's**
specializing in family-group river tours
Phone (250) 752-3149

## Fishing Tackle Shops

**Alberni Seafood & Tackle**
Phone (250) 723-9333

**Gone Fishin'**
open daily at 8 a.m.
Phone (250) 723-1172

# Accommodations

## CAMPGROUNDS
**Timber Lodge and RV Campground**
Port Alberni
Phone (250) 723-9415

**Stamp River Provincial Park** — on the river
Phone (250) 954-4600

**China Creek Marina and Campground**
Port Alberni
Phone (250) 723-9812

**Galaxy Way Campground**
at the end of McKenzie Road, on the Stamp River

## FISHING LODGES & RESORTS
**Eagle Nook Wilderness Resort**
Port Alberni
Phone (250) 723-1000

**Riverside Lodge**
B&B, Port Alberni
Phone (250) 723-3474

## HOTELS & MOTELS
**Best Western Barclay Hotel**
Port Alberni
(250) 724-7171

**Coast Hospitality Inn**
(250) 723-8111

**Somass Motel**
(800) 927-2217

**Sunset Motel**
(250) 723-2231

**Tyee Village Motel**
(800) 663-6676 or (250) 723-4798

# Distances to Stamp River

**From:**

- Vancouver, BC — 110 km (68 miles)
- Blaine, WA USA border — 130 km (81 miles)
- Calgary, AB — 1065 km (661 miles)
- Edmonton, AB — 1245 km (773 miles)

(Distances shown do not include the ferry trip from the mainland to Vancouver Island.)

# BC Ferries Information

### From Mainland BC to Vancouver Island

- Phone 1-888-223-3779 toll free from anywhere in BC
- Fax (250) 381-5452 for reservations
- Vancouver Island routes: phone 1-888-724-5223 toll free in BC / (604) 444-2890 if you call from outside BC
- Ferry travel information on the Internet: www.bcferries.com

Stamp River.                    Photo: Bob Tustin

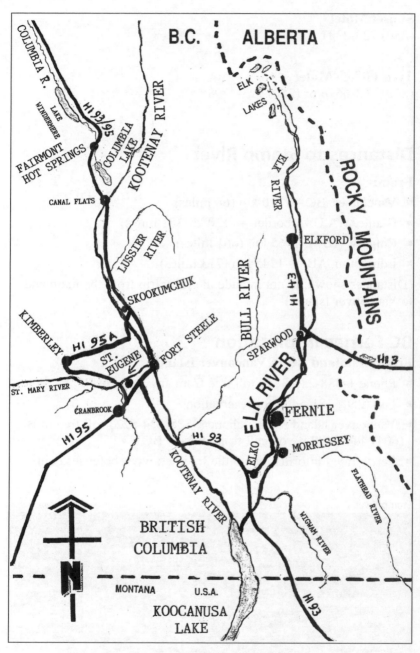

**Rockies/Kootenay Region**

CHAPTER 13

# Elk River in the Canadian Rockies
plus the St. Mary River

> *There are two kinds of anglers: those who live in British Columbia, and those who wish they did.*
> — ROBERT H. JONES

I do believe that Mr. Robert H. Jones probably is quite correct. When Pauline and I were fishing, camping and photographing along the Elk River, we met more Albertan anglers than British Columbian anglers. This really isn't difficult to understand when you consider that the Elk River is 965 kilometers from Vancouver, BC, but it is only 280 kilometers from the busy city of Calgary, Alberta.

There are no large metropolitan centers in the Elk River Valley, but the Elk's "big town" is Fernie (population 4,877). In spite of its small population, this Rocky Mountain community has hotels, motels, RV parks, resorts, lodges, bed-and-breakfasts, hostels and campgrounds. The stores in town cater to the needs of visitors—visiting anglers, hikers, nature lovers and all other tourists. Transportation isn't a problem in Fernie—you can hop on a Greyhound Bus in town and ride to anyplace in North America.

The history of Fernie is a chronicle of catastrophes and recoveries.

In the early days of Fernie's infamous Coal Creek Mine, working and living conditions were pitiful, if not downright criminal. Child labor existed in the coal mine until 1920. Disastrous accidents were commonplace. On May 20, 1902, the Coal Creek Mine received its customary inspection and the mine was pronounced safe. Yet, two days later, on May 22, a deafening explosion thundered out of num-

Gordon Davies near the mouth of the Elk River.

ber two colliery. A hundred and twenty-eight men died in that blast, many of whom remain buried forever.

In Fernie on August 1, 1908, at two o'clock in the afternoon, a wind of hurricane velocity spread flames from a smoldering bonfire to the sawmill of the Cedar Valley Lumber Company. The fire consumed the mill in minutes; the flames raced through the commercial and residential areas of Fernie. At least ten people perished in the fire, and the town lay in ruins.

Within a few weeks the determined citizens returned and erected a tent town; in a year the city was rebuilt, mainly of brick. Residents of Fernie are a tough, resilient lot. In 1957, a half-century after the Great Fire, when the Coal Creek Mine ceased operations forever, the prophets of doom predicted that Fernie would soon become a ghost town. But they didn't reckon with the faith and grit of the people of Fernie who refused to desert their hometown. And, as we can see today, the stubborn, optimistic citizens and their town are here to stay, no longer relying solely on mining but turning instead to tourism and other sources of income.

If you are a river angler and you are visiting Fernie, and if you are contemplating some fishing in the Elk River, here is the name of a great fishing guide who lives in town: Kim Sedrovic, who resides at 9 Ridgemont Avenue, Fernie. You can phone him at (250) 423-6704. Kim's mailing address is listed in the "Who is What?" Section at the end of this chapter.

From what I have seen along the length of the Elk River, the lower reaches, between the Highway 93 Bridge and the mouth of the big waterway at Koocanusa Lake, appear to be the best bet for anglers seeking really big fish. Some awesome Dolly Varden are caught here. One afternoon while I was shooting scenic photos near the river mouth, an angler beached four Dollies, all in the three- to five-pound class. He kept one and released the others but, evidently, these really were not large Dollies by Elk River standards. I knew there were six- to seven-pounders in the lower river, but one day in the Gold Creek Sportstore in Cranbrook, Paul Panchyshyn told me that eight- to fourteen-pounders have been caught there—and another Elk River angler claimed some reach weights of up to 20 pounds. I wouldn't suggest that fishermen exaggerate, but perhaps 20 pounds is a slight overestimation. Some anglers launch their small boats in Koocanusa Lake at the rivermouth, where they troll for large Dolly Varden.

At its headwaters, the fish-rich Elk River is an alpine trout stream, originating high in the Canadian Rocky Mountains. For me, the phrase "alpine trout stream" always conjures up a mental picture of a babbling brook tumbling down a hillside—a friendly little creek with a small population of five-inch trout. Well, I want you to know that some alpine trout streams just don't fit this description at all! For example, look at the magnificent Elk, British Columbia's most easterly river. For most of its length the Elk is a big, boisterous, brawling river—and many of its cutthroat trout and Dolly Varden char are big, boisterous and brawling too! Access to this waterway is surprisingly easy—by road or good trail—along much of its length.

High in the glacier-strewn Rockies where the Elk River flows out of Lower Elk Lake, the bighorn sheep, elk, moose and grizzly bears roam among the spruce and fir trees, while tall lodgepole pines reach skyward, straining to touch the clouds. Early summer daytime temperatures can reach seventy to eighty degrees Fahrenheit at the headwaters of the Elk, but the mercury can drop below the freezing mark at night—in the summer! So you'd better not plan an early springtime trout-fishing junket to the upper Elk River in March or April. In fact, it might be better if you didn't even think about going in May or June either. The middle of July, after the high water has dropped, should be a comfortable time for a visit.

Summer arrives late at the upper reaches of the Elk River, and its arrival is accompanied by an explosion of bright rainbow-hued wildflowers. Hillsides are ablaze with violets, white rhododendrons, false azalea and bunchberries; the alpine meadows are carpeted with ragwort, lupines, fireweed and Indian paintbrush. In mid-summer the upper Elk River Valley is a paradise for hikers, campers and all nature lovers.

Hemmed in on both sides by towering white-topped mountains, the Elk River flows south through lonely wild forests to the modern coal-mining town of Elkford, the community that calls itself the "Wilderness Capital of British Columbia."

Upstream and downstream from Elkford there is good trout water. Line Creek Bridge below Elkford is a favorite spot. There are days when an angler can stroll up and down this part of the Elk River without encountering another human being. After all, there is plenty of elbow room on this big stream and, luckily, the Elk is remote enough to escape the weekend invasions of most big-city anglers.

The Elk River at Elkford.

When the spring freshet subsides and the water clears up a little, the great Elk River offers some excellent light tackle fishing. Cutthroat trout up to three pounds and Dolly Varden char weighing in excess of five pounds may be taken on flies and lures in summer and early autumn. Mountain whitefish angling starts in earnest when the bait ban is lifted on the first day of November.

A town of three thousand residents, nestled in the middle of an unspoiled alpine wilderness, Elkford was born in 1970. Nearby rich coal deposits gave birth to this Rocky Mountain community, whose cleanliness and neatness contrast sharply with the smoky-gray dinginess and the overcrowding of the drab old Elk Valley coal towns of the early twentieth century. Elkford's ex-mayor, Jack White, will tell you that his town has the world's finest scenery, and forests that support more wild game than any other place in North America. White will also tell you that the sight of a grizzly bear wandering casually through downtown Elkford is not at all unusual.

The next community on our trek downstream is Sparwood, the home of Canada's largest open pit coal mine. A few miles down the river from Sparwood is the ghost town of Hosmer with a colorful

The Elk River.

past that dates back to the early 1900s when coal mining was Hosmer's biggest (and only) industry. A large part of the community's residential district was destroyed in the Elk Valley's Great Fire of 1908, but the coal mine survived unscathed. In July, 1914, the mining operation was closed down and ninety-nine per cent of Hosmer's residents left town.

Although there are many breathtaking vistas throughout the valley of the Elk, the panoramic view from the old Hosmer townsite, looking across the waters of the rolling river to the towering white-frosted Rocky Mountains is one of the most strikingly beautiful sights in the area. And there is more than spectacular scenery at the ghost town of Hosmer. There is plenty of productive trout water here that can be fished from both the west side of the river and the east side.

Moving down the Elk River, we come once again to the Elk Valley's big town, Fernie, the home of the veteran whitefish angler Terry Zuffa. Although whitefish can be caught on flies and small lures, the vast majority are taken on bait, particularly single salmon eggs, hellgrammites and maggots. There is a bait ban on the Elk during the summer and early fall months, but this prohibition is lifted on the first day of November, allowing whitefish anglers to use natural bait. Elk River whitefish are quite easily caught in the late fall and winter by fishermen who can tolerate low air temperatures. Daily catch limit is fifteen fish. Terry Zuffa loves to catch whitefish and, believe me, he is successful at the sport. He has been fishing in the Elk River Valley since he was a boy in the 1940s, and he has a very practical reason for wanting to catch whitefish. Mrs. Zuffa uses the meat to make the world's tastiest fish cakes. Terry tells me that the making of the famous fish cakes is a simple matter—just scale the fish, decapitate it, gut it, boil it, scrape the meat off the bones, then use the meat to make the fish cakes. If you really want a detailed recipe, you'll just have to contact Mrs. Zuffa. Personally, I never learned how to cook anything, but I was truly grateful to learn about the fish cakes from Terry Zuffa, because my wife has been searching for forty years to find a practical way to prepare the meat of these bony fish.

Between Fernie and the downstream community of Elko, the river is dramatically scenic, accessible, often uncrowded, and productive. While pursuing the Elk's handsome cutthroat trout along this stretch of the stream, an angler finds some priceless bonuses—an opportunity to relax and breathe deeply of the fresh, clean mountain air, to contemplate the regal grandeur of the Rockies, and simply to be alive in the superb, scenic valley of the Elk.

Early one evening I was shooting some photos of a fly fisherman as he waded through a shallow stretch near mid-stream. Later, while we were making camp at the riverside, this fly caster stopped by to visit us, introduced himself as John Poirier of Fernie and kindly presented us with a fat cutthroat trout that provided us with a tasty lunch the following day. A fine gentleman, an ardent fishing enthusiast and a true sportsman, John fly fishes his home river, the Elk, at every possible opportunity.

In 1902 on the banks of the Elk River, south of Fernie, a coal mine, a newspaper, several hotels, some stores, a church and two towns appeared, flourished for a brief moment, then disappeared as suddenly as they had come. The two towns were named Morrissey and Morrissey Mines. The coal mine that spawned all the urban development was a total failure from the start.

Upon learning that the coal in the region was of very low quality, the mine owners fled, and everything collapsed. Today, in the vicinity of the two ill-fated coal towns, travelers can stop and enjoy a rest at the Morrissey Picnic Grounds on the west bank of the beautiful Elk River. On a sunny summer day in the late 1980s, Pauline and I drove in and parked at the little Morrissey Picnic Grounds. We prowled around this part of the stream, made a few casts, shot some photos, then decided to drive up the river to Fernie. I opened the door of our truck-camper and tossed in our camera bags, tripods and fishing tackle. I drove a couple of miles upriver, spotted a particularly scenic spot and pulled off the road to take some pictures. But when I opened the camper door to reach for a camera, I noticed that Pauline's favorite fishing rod was missing. And then, with a sickening shock, I remembered! Back at Morrissey I had leaned her rod and reel against the back of the camper, intending to put them inside before we drove off. Damn! In a panic, and feeling more than somewhat stupid, because I knew for certain that I had left her rod and reel behind, I got in behind the wheel, made a U-turn and drove straight back to Morrissey. Not more than fifteen minutes had elapsed since we left. The picnic ground was empty when we left and nobody was there when we returned, but Pauline's favorite rod was gone. She assured me, "It's not important. Don't worry about it." Well, maybe it didn't matter to her but believe me, I felt terrible about the incident until I found a similar graphite rod and bought it (and a new reel) for her before we left the Elk Valley.

At the village of Elko on the lower river there is a small hydro-electric dam—not a tall structure, but high enough to prevent downstream fish from ascending into the upper river. In addition to cutthroat trout, Dolly Varden char and mountain whitefish, there were (and still may be) a few eastern brook trout in the river near Elko. Some of these brook trout were known to reach two pounds in weight. Below the dam and all the way to the river mouth at Koocanusa Lake, an angler may encounter rainbows, cutthroat and large Dollies that have moved in from the lake.

Above the BC-Montana Highway (93) Bridge there is a big canyon. Except for the highway, the only access to other parts of this deep canyon is via primitive back roads. The overview of the Elk River Canyon from a high point near Cutts Road is overwhelming. This part of the gorge is so deep and steep that the high canyon rim actually blocks out the sun in the depths below for most of the day. A short distance downstream from the Highway 93 Bridge, the Elk River empties into Koocanusa Lake. If you are interested in a mess of small but exceedingly tasty panfish, there are plenty of kokanee (freshwater sockeye salmon) in Koocanusa Lake. In the 1970s several hundred kokanee fry escaped into the Bull River from the Kootenay Fish Hatchery. They migrated down the Bull River into the waters of Koocanusa Lake where they found an abundance of food and ideal spawning streams. To say the self-transplanted kokanee are doing well in their new home would be a gross understatement. The couple of hundred kokanee that moved into the lake in the 1970s grew to 2,500,000 by the 1990s. And the daily catch limit on kokanees is ten fish!

So there you have it, the incomparable Elk River—from the peaks of the Canadian Rockies to Koocanusa Lake—a truly magnificent alpine trout stream! If you are planning to visit this fine, fish-rich waterway, I hope you tie into some big, fat Dolly Varden or hard-fighting cutthroat trout—or a mess of whitefish, so you can cook up some fish cakes a la Mrs. Terry Zuffa.

# What's where ?
## And where is what ?

## Gamefish Species
Dolly Varden char, cutthroat trout, mountain whitefish and (in Koocanusa Lake) kokanee.

# Regulations and Restrictions

### Elk River above Elko Dam
- Bait ban June 15 to Oct. 31.
- Trout and char release from June 15 to Oct. 31.
- from Lower Elk Lake to Forsyth Creek
- from Line Creek Bridge to CPR Bridge at Sparwood.
- from the Highway 3 Bridge at Hosmer to the northern Highway 3 Bridge at Fernie
- and from the bridge at Morrissey to Elko Dam

### All other parts of Elk River above Elko Dam
- Trout and char: daily limit one.
- No cutthroat under 30 cm.
- No Dollies under 75 cm.

### Below Elko Dam
- Trout and char: daily limit one. No trout under 30 cm. No Dollies under 75 cm. The Elk's Dolly Varden are huge and minimum length is 20.5 inches.
- Mountain whitefish: 15 per day.

### Tributaries of the Elk River
- Closed to fishing Sept. 1 to Oct. 31.
- Daily catch limit, June 15 to August 31: one. None under 30 cm.

### Exceptions for tributaries of the Elk River
- Alexander Creek above Highway 3: trout/char release and bait ban June 15 to Aug. 31. No fishing Sept. 1 to Oct. 31.
- Abruzzi Creek: same as Alexander.
- Bighorn (Ram) Creek: Fly fishing only. Bait Ban. Trout/char release June 15 to Sept. 15. Closed Sept. 16 to Oct. 31.
- Cadorna Creek: No fishing Sept. 1 to Oct. 31. Trout/char release. Bait ban, June 13 to Aug. 31.

- Fording Creek below Josephine Falls: Trout/char release. Bait ban June 15 to Oct. 31.
- Forsyth Creek closed from Connor Lake downstream three kilometers.

**Wigwam River**

- A tributary of the Elk, is the home of big cutthroat trout. Requires a one-hour hike through wild bush, plenty of bears (bring a can of bear spray and don't hike into the Wigwam alone.) Fly fishing only and bait ban. Closed above Bighorn (Ram) Creek Sept. 16 to Oct. 31. Bait ban.
- Line Creek: closed to fishing.
- Morrissey Creek: Closed Sept. 1 to Oct. 31. Trout/char release.
- Lodgepole Creek: Closed Sept. 16 to Oct. 31.
- Below falls near km 26: Trout/char release June 15 to Sept. 15. Bait ban, fly fishing only.
- Michel Creek below Highway 3: Trout/char one per day, none under 30 cm. Bait ban. Catch and release June 15 to Oct. 31.

For more information or clarification on regulations and restrictions phone (250) 489-8540 and visit BC Fisheries website: www.bcfisheries.gov.bc.ca

# Angling Methods

The Elk is an excellent fly-fishing river, particularly for its great cutthroat trout. However, if you're going after its large Dolly Varden char, you'll find spinning rods or other casting tackle appropriate for tossing Krocodile, Five of Diamonds or Gibbs Koho spoons.

- **Trout Flies:** Anderson's Rubber Leg Stone, Gold-Ribbed Hare's Ear Nymph, Ausable Wulff, Mosquito, a selection of stone fly and caddis patterns, Parachute Adams, Tom Thumb, Coachman, Muddler Minnow, Grizzly King, Black Gnat, Green Sedge and every other pattern of trout fly that you have faith in.

- **Lures:** Small and medium-size Krocodile Spoons, in various colors. Five-of-Diamonds spoons, Dardevle spoons, Flatfish plugs, small weighted spinners.
- **Baits:** When the bait ban is lifted on November 1, small natural baits are most effective for mountain whitefish. Use tiny hooks for live maggots and preserved (bottled) single salmon eggs.

## Fishing Guides for the Elk River System

**Fernie Wilderness Adventure**
9 Ridgemont Avenue, Fernie, BC, Canada V0B 1M2
Phone (250) 423-6704, Fax (250) 423-6717

Kim Sedrovic, proprietor, will give you a great fishing guide to take you to the fishiest spots in the Elk River Valley.

## Accommodations

**Elkford Motor Inn**
808 Michel Road, Box 1060, Elkford, BC V0B 1H0
Phone (250) 865-2211.

**Hi Rock Inn**
Box 1267, Elkford, BC V0B 1H0

**Kikomun Creek Provincial Park**
Phone (250) 422-4200

**West Crow Motel & RV Park**
Box 1000, Elko, BC V0B 1J0
Phone (250) 529-7349

**Mount Fernie Provincial Park**
Highway 3, west of Fernie

Fly fishing near the mouth of Matthew Creek, St. Mary River.

**Raging Elk Hostel**
Quiet location, seniors discount
Box 1899, Fernie, BC V0B 1M0
Phone (250) 423-6811

# Highway Distances to Elk River

**From:**

- Vancouver, BC — 965 km (599 miles)
- Blaine, WA USA border — 960 km (596 miles)
- Calgary, AB — 280 km (174 miles)
- Edmonton, AB — 575 km (357 miles)

McPhee Bridge area of the St. Mary River.

## A Lovely Trout Stream — St. Mary River

The St. Mary is a fine, almost-wild waterway that offers excellent fly fishing for cutthroat trout, rainbow trout, Dolly Varden char and a hybrid, sterile, artificial cutthroat-rainbow they call a "cuttbow." To drive to the St. Mary from the Elk River, you follow Highway 3/93 to Fort Steele or Wycliffe on the St. Mary River.

Access to much of this gorgeous trout stream is almost impossible without a boat and a local fishing guide (almost essential on the river). But don't let this deter you—just drive to the town of Kimberley on Mark Creek, a tributary of the St. Mary, where you will find the St. Mary Angler and Guiding Service. This company has excellent fishing guides and sells suitable tackle for the St. Mary River. Phone toll free 1-800-667-2311. Their mailing address is: No. 1, 340 Mark Street, Kimberley, BC V1A 3A1.

And here is a conveniently located campground: Happy Hans Campground and RV Park (141 sites), on the St. Mary River Road. Phone (250) 427-2929 or (250) 427-4877.

# CHAPTER 14

# Non-Stop Action on the Vedder
plus the Lower Fraser Valley

*Fishermen are born honest, but they get over it.* — ED ZERN

B ased on a thirty-year average (1971 to 2000) the Vedder is the most productive steelhead river in British Columbia. We can thank God and the Vedder's fish hatchery for this river's tremendous steelhead and salmon fishing. The fish hatchery in the Slesse Creek area has been incredibly successful, producing eleven million salmon smolts each year, including chinook, coho and chum. This hatchery also produces great numbers of steelhead from wild brood stock.

The remarkable Vedder (alias Chilliwack) River attracts anglers from every part of the North American continent and a few from the other side of the globe. This incredibly popular waterway boasts autumn runs of approximately 100,000 chinook and 50,000 coho salmon. The Vedder also has an exceptional steelhead fishery that allows anglers to keep hatchery steelhead, while releasing all wild steelhead. And here is some good news, there is easy road access into most of this great river.

Winter steelheading is the sport that made the Vedder River famous. Upon seeing this river for the first time—its clean gravel bottom, its whitewater runs and its picture-perfect pools—an experienced river fisher knows instinctively that this wonderful stream is, in every way, a classic steelhead river. Each year around Christmas and New Year's Day, great hordes of anglers from all over the lower mainland of BC descend upon the river. All the well-known pools and runs are subjected to a heavy assault during the holiday season. The fishing action slows down in late January to mid-February when many of the steelheaders pack it in for the season. But some veteran fishermen return to the river to fish the late steelhead run that arrives in March, and sometimes provides good sport well into the month of April.

When steelhead are migrating up the Vedder River, the great waterway becomes extremely crowded. Shoulder-to-shoulder fishing is not a lot of fun—and this is precisely why some steelheaders who don't enjoy togetherness have developed a system (I learned of it in the 1960s) that frequently pays off. This system isn't difficult to master. Some Vedder veterans simply do not fish in the well-known runs and pools. They search out small pockets between the heavily fished waters. Good holding water can be found in some very unlikely places. Even in fastwater rapids there are some depressions in the bottom (often behind very large boulders) that provide resting places for steelhead. Some of these hard-to-locate spots can hold two or more fish.

When you find some of these hidden fish-holding pockets, there is no guarantee you will be able to coax the fish into striking, but it certainly beats fishing in a crowd, especially when you are well aware that the big pools have been worked over since dawn by dozens of other anglers.

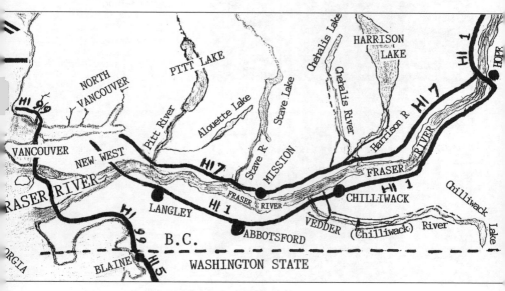

**Lower Mainland Region**

White clouds, high mountains and fast water — an ideal setting for the contemplative angler. The Vedder is a truly beautiful river in a majestic setting.

Winter steelheading can be a very cold business. It is no accident that winter anglers wear long johns, heavy wool socks, Cowichan Indian sweaters and weatherproof parkas. Diehard winter steelheaders have been described as "determined, indomitable and dedicated." I have no argument with these adjectives, but occasionally I have thought that words like "stubborn, foolhardy, obstinate" or just plain "crazy" might be more appropriate. In all this world, there just cannot be any other type of sport fishing as tough and challenging as the finger-freezing game known as winter steelheading.

A valid aesthetic reason for the Vedder's popularity is the fact that it is a truly splendid river in a magnificent scenic setting. In the high, conifer-forested hills southeast of Chilliwack, BC, this superb river flows from the deep waters of Chilliwack Lake. In a procession of tumbling, frothing rapids, interspersed with mirror-surfaced stretches, the great stream cuts a winding swath through the Skagit Range of the Cascade Mountains as it descends to the valley floor. After absorbing several tributary creeks and the flow from half a dozen tiny lakes, the river winds its way through small farms, advancing steadily through the outskirts of the village of Vedder Crossing. It then slides through the artificial confines of a man-made canal and is joined by the Sumas River, before being swallowed up by British Columbia's largest waterway, the muddy Fraser River.

This splendid river actually changes its name as it flows under a bridge. Above the bridge at Vedder Crossing it is the Chilliwack River, below the bridge it is the Vedder River.

There is an explanation—but never could it be called a logical reason for this en route name-change. Early in the twentieth century, when drainage canals were created for flood control, the lower Chilliwack River was diverted into a newly excavated channel. This new channel (from the bridge at Vedder Crossing downstream) was re-named the Vedder River. But upstream of the bridge it retained its original name, Chilliwack River. This curious situation enables an angler to perform a seemingly impossible feat. Standing in one spot, he can hook a fish in the Vedder River, then land it on the bank of the Chilliwack River.

The new channel was christened "Vedder River" in honor of two early settlers, Adam and Volkert Vedder. However, many British Columbia river fishers refer to the entire river, from source to mouth, as "the Vedder."

Autumn is coho salmon time on the Vedder, and the fishing can be terrific, thanks mainly to the impressive returns of hatchery fish. Coho anglers can usually count on tolerable weather. Most of the time it is actually sunny and warm but now and then it can be cool, windy, rainy or foggy, and more than somewhat uncomfortable.

Below the Vedder Crossing Bridge and above the bridge to the upstream fishing boundary at Slesse Creek there is plenty of ideal holding water for the coho salmon. In the fall, even after an extremely hot summer, there is sufficient water to offer some protection to migrating cohos. The Vedder in autumn appears to be a river fisherman's paradise. The deciduous trees are clothed in their brilliant red and gold fall colors, the salmon are moving upriver on their spawning run, and there are many miles of fishable pools to explore. It all sounds too good to be true and, in one respect, it is. The Vedder suffers from one extremely serious problem: too damn many anglers!

Every river fisher in southwestern British Columbia knows the reputation of the splendid Vedder River and its outstanding coho salmon runs, and there are days on the river when it looks like every one of these anglers has arrived at the same time. But this does not necessarily mean you must abandon your plans to fish the river for coho. Fortunately, there are several things you can do to reduce the possibility of encountering a large crowd at riverside. Start fishing near Slesse Creek, about five miles above Vedder Crossing, and work your way downstream. You should find less competition on this stretch of water, because many anglers prefer to fish the pools and runs within a mile or so of Vedder Crossing.

River fishers who are not averse to scrambling over a boulder-strewn shore can enjoy some fine fishing below the Tamihi Bridge, halfway between Slesse Creek and Vedder Crossing. On a sunny September morning I was perched on a large rock downstream from the bridge, surveying the splendid river and the wondrous, fragile handiwork of Mother Nature. A breeze rustled the bushes at streamside, a salmon surfaced in the slow run below me, and I realized once again how fortunate I am to live in British Columbia, the land of great rivers.

If your working schedule allows it, avoid fishing the Vedder on weekends and holidays. You'll see far fewer fishermen on a cloudy weekday morning than you'll see on a sunny Saturday afternoon. Because the Vedder is an easy stream for wading anglers, it is a

Vedder River above village of Vedder Crossing.

The Vedder River near Tamihi Creek.

favorite haunt of many skilled West Coast river fishers. Along the banks of this marvelous waterway you are certain to meet some of these typical BC stream fishermen with their nine- to twelve-foot rods and their Hardy Silex or level-wind casting reels.

Accommodation, meals and tackle for visiting anglers are available at or near the community of Vedder Crossing. At this friendly little village there are campgrounds, rental cabins, restaurants, a pharmacy, hardware and grocery stores. When you are in Vedder Crossing, be sure you visit one of Canada's most successful river anglers, Fred Helmer, at his fine tackle shop, "Fred's Custom Tackle." Many moons ago, when he was a mere youngster, Fred subdued an eight-hundred-pound-plus sturgeon while angling in British Columbia's big Fraser River. For knowledgeable, accurate information on local angling, drop in and see Fred in beautiful downtown Vedder Crossing.

In addition to salmon and steelhead, there are some other important species of game fish in the Vedder River—most importantly, rainbow and cutthroat trout and Dolly Varden char. One of our finest freshwater sport fish, the native coastal cutthroat can give the angler a spirited battle when it is caught on light tackle. The Dolly Varden char, unfairly maligned by some fishermen, has often meant the difference between a productive fishing trip and a complete skunking.

Dolly Varden is an intriguing and unusual name for a species of fish. Also intriguing and unusual is the story behind the adoption of its name. The original Dolly Varden was a young lady in a popular Charles Dickens novel. A drygoods manufacturer named a colorfully spotted new calico material "Dolly Varden" after the character in the story. The spotted calico material became quite famous, and so did the Dolly Varden name. Upon visiting the early western frontier, a sophisticated lady from the enlightened east saw one of the brightly spotted western char and remarked on its striking resemblance to the stylish Dolly Varden calico. Hence the name of our colorfully-spotted western char.

What a great bit of history, tying our fish legitimately to the renowned nineteenth century author Charles Dickens! And a pox on those troublemakers nowadays who would have us call them "bull trout"! Migawd! They aren't even trout!

How does the Vedder retain its perennial popularity among the fishing fraternity? A fair question, considering the fact that its salmon and steelhead runs have suffered from varying degrees of degradation and depletion over the last fifty years, and heavy angling pressure often creates uncomfortable shoulder-to-shoulder fishing conditions. Major flooding occurred on the Vedder in late autumn of 1989, 1990 and 1991, causing severe damage to homes, farmland, tourist recreation areas, roads and salmon spawning grounds. Some informed observers, like well-known Chilliwack outdoorsman James Griffin, believe these destructive fall floods are the result of irresponsible clear-cut logging practices.

One major reason for the Vedder River's continued popularity is the simple fact that it is located within easy driving distance of the big city of Vancouver. Additionally, in spite of fluctuations in fish populations, the Vedder still provides some surprisingly good fishing for coho salmon in the fall, steelhead in the winter, and the occasional cutthroat or Dolly Varden at any time of the year. Almost all the good pools on the river can be reached by automobile, and the rest of the fishy water can be accessed by trails. Whether you are camping along the river in midsummer or fishing in the fall, winter or spring, you can readily appreciate why the noble, glorious Vedder is southern British Columbia's favorite river.

But what about the overcrowding?

Well, just remember what one wise man, veteran B. C. steelheader Big Ed Kendall says: "If you're going to fish the Vedder, you'd better take your own rock to stand on."

# What's where ?
# And where is what ?

## Gamefish Species and Seasons

All salmon open July 1 to March 31.

- **Chinook Salmon** (spring, king, chinook, quinnat): Daily limit of 4, only one over 62 cm.
- **Chum Salmon** (dog salmon): Daily catch limit of 1.
- **Coho Salmon** (silver salmon): Season—autumn. Daily catch limit of 4.
- **Steelhead:** Daily catch limit, 1 hatchery fish / 0 wild fish. Season, approximately mid-December to early April.
- **Rainbow Trout, Cutthroat Trout and Dolly Varden Char:** Cutthroat spawn in the spring and Dollies are fall-spawners, but either of these species may move into the river at any time of the year.

## Restrictions

- Single barbless hook
- Closed to fishing above (and including) Slesse Creek, year-round.
- Closed to fishing May 1 to June 30, below Slesse Creek to Vedder Crossing.
- Wild trout and Dolly Varden release.
- Hatchery rainbow trout, any length 50 cm or less. Daily limit 4.

For more information on fishing regulations:

- Phone (604) 702-2278 or (604) 582-5200
- www.bcfisheries.gov.ca

# Angling Methods

- **British Columbia Coast-Style Float Fishing (bobber fishing):** This old bait-fishing method involves using a plastic, foam or cork float (bobber) and a long leader that allows the bait to drift along near the bottom (sometimes even bumping the bottom).
- **Fly fishing and casting artificial lures.**
- **Artificial Lures for Steelhead:** Krocodile spoons, Gooey Bobs, Spin-n-Glos, Gibbs Koho spoons.
- **Steelhead Flies—A Few Proven Patterns:** Skunk, Umpqua, Practitioner, Black Practitioner, Cowichan Special, Coquihalla Orange, Squamish Poacher, and hundreds more.
- **Coho Flies:** Coho Blue, Clouser, Lioness, Fall Favorite, Coho Sunset, Pearl Mickey Finn, Chartreuse Popsicle, Coho Peacock plus any patterns recommended by the folks at Fred's Custom Tackle in the village of Vedder Crossing.

# Guides, Outfitters, Charters, River Tours

**Fred's Fishing Adventures** — Friendly Guides
No. 1, 5580 Vedder Road, Chilliwack, BC V2R 5P4
Phone 604-858-7344
www.freds-bc.com

**Fishing Tackle Shop**
Fred's Custom Tackle at Vedder Crossing
No. 1, 5580 Vedder Road, Chilliwack, BC V2R 5P4
Phone 604-858-7344

# Accommodations

**Riverside Resort Ltd.** (since 1920)
Restaurant, cabins, fishing guide
45530 Vedder Mountain Road, Chilliwack, BC V2R 4C3

**Chilliwack River Campground**
50801 O'Byrne Road
Phone (604) 858-4443

**Vedder River Campground**
5215 Giesbrecht Road
Phone (604) 823-6012
Fax (604) 823-6048

**Forest Service Recreation Sites**
There are nine rather inexpensive Forest Service recreation sites along the Vedder-Chilliwack River between Chilliwack Lake and Vedder Crossing. Seven of these offer overnight camping.

Highway Distances to the Vedder (Chilliwack) River

**From:**

- Vancouver, BC — 114 km (71miles)
- Blaine, WA USA border — 105 km (65 miles)
- Calgary, AB — 792 km (492 miles)
- Edmonton, AB — 1041 km (646 miles)

# Monster Fish of the Lower Fraser River

Just a stone's throw away from the Vedder River there is an opportunity for you to participate in some unusual, exciting, incredible big game fishing in the lower reaches of the mighty Fraser River, albeit totally catch-and-release. The white sturgeon—a fish that has existed since the days of the dinosaurs—is a hard-fighting critter that can weigh 300 to 800 pounds, but 100- to 200-pounders are more common. However, confirmed world record size is 1,800 pounds and 20 feet in length. If you wish to hook some sturgeon, you must accept the fact that your chances are excellent only if you hire a professional, successful sturgeon-fishing guide. Here are some of the best. Be sure to check for possible sturgeon angling closure.

Sturgeon in Lower Fraser River.

*Photo: Gill's Tackle & Guiding Service*

**Brent Gill, Fishing Guide**
**Gill's Fishing Tackle**
No. 4, 19300 Number Ten Highway (Langley Bypass)
Surrey, BC V3S 6K2
Phone (604) 530-6266

**Tony Nooteboss, Fishing Guide**
**Harrison Bay Guiding Services**
140 Esplanade Ave., Harrison Hot Springs, V0M 1K0
Phone (604) 796-3345, Cell Phone (604) 312-8070

**Fred Helmer, Fishing Guide**
**Fred's Fishing Adventures**
No. 1, 5580 Vedder Road, Chilliwack, BC V2R 5P4
Phone (604) 858-7344

# Fraser River Bar Fishing

Here is a little info on a very popular style of angling on the mighty Fraser.

Many moons ago, when I was a kid in New Westminster, I caught my first sea-run trout (a silver-bright Fraser River cutthroat) while fishing from a sandbar on Lulu Island. I'll never forget the panic when I hooked that fish! I grabbed my hand line securely and ran up the bar, a hundred yards from the water's edge, dragging the trout out of the river until it lay flopping on the sand. Finesse wasn't part of my technique in those days!

But I had my trout in hand, and at that moment I joined a unique angling fraternity—the bar fishermen of the Fraser.

Fraser River bar fishermen (and fisherwomen) are the most relaxed, friendly, optimistic and patient anglers on earth. On the sandbars of 'Old Muddy,' from Yale downstream to Steveston, these easy-going outdoorsmen cast their baits into the river, prop their rods on sand spikes, recline in their lawn chairs, sip their beer, listen to their portable radios, and wait for a bite from a trout or salmon.

Comfort is the key to bar fishing. Any bar fisherman worth his salt will be equipped with a camp stove, groceries, beverages, snacks, coffee, tea, lawn chair, foot stool, blankets, pillows, umbrella, portable television, reading material and sunglasses. An indispensable accessory for the dedicated sandbar angler is a small bell that attaches to his rod tip and emits an audible signal when a fish nibbles at his bait. Without a bell, an angler might feel obliged to remain awake—and this could become extremely tiring. Access into the sandbars is easy via roads suitable for motor vehicles.

CHAPTER **15**

# Harrison — The Trouter's River

*The true sportsman is one who not only will not show his own father where the best fishing hole is, but will deliberately direct him to the wrong one.*

— GREGORY CLARK

The wide Harrison River pours out of Harrison Lake near the world-famous lakeside town of Harrison Hot Springs which, with its hotels, motels, recreational vehicle parks, unique boutiques, souvenir shops and gourmet restaurants, is thoroughly tourist-oriented. In addition to soaking in the stimulating waters of Harrison's mineral-rich natural hot springs, visitors enjoy swimming in the azure waters of the lake and sunbathing on clean sandy beaches. They windsurf and play golf and tennis while enjoying the magnificent splendor of a backdrop of green-forested hills and snow-crowned mountains.

Although Harrison Hot Springs is, for good reason, the most-visited, most popular spot in the entire region, there is another lovely little place a few miles downstream from the hot-spring-spa town that attracts far fewer tourists but far more trout fishers—Kilby's friendly, laid-back, rustic provincial park and beach-front campground on Harrison Bay. Situated at a particularly wide spot on the river facing out across the waters of Harrison Bay (it looks more like a lake than a bay), Kilby Park is ideal for people like Pauline and me, where we can rough it in comfort while enjoying a sweeping vista of water, winged wildlife, and every type of craft from kayak to tugboat.

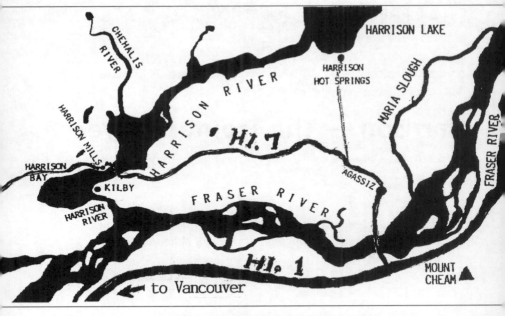

**Harrison Region of British Columbia**

Within easy walking distance of the campground is an unusual museum, incorporating the original old Kilby General Store and several other historic buildings with antique furnishings—an ancient boarding house, post office, milk house, and even an authentic old-fashioned hand-operated ice cream machine and a vintage cider press.

In the autumn and in the springtime, when trout fishing is at its best, the long stretch of sandy beach at Kilby Park can be a beehive of activity. Anglers launch boats here, then head for less accessible fishing spots upstream, above the highway bridge. The Harrison's slow, steady current doesn't look very powerful, but it is stronger than it appears to be, and shouldn't be challenged in an underpowered boat. The trip up the blue-green river takes boaters through Harrison Rapids, near the mouth of its most important tributary, the famous, fishy Chehalis River, and past the mouth of Morris Creek, on the way upriver to Harrison Lake.

There is no public road access to the mouth of the Harrison River, but boats launched at Kilby Park can run downriver to the stream's confluence with the mighty, muddy Fraser River.

On sunny days in late spring and early fall, I have watched groups of chest-wadered fly fishers standing waist deep in the water at Kilby, laying out long perfectly-cast lines, while behind them on the sandy beach, children were playing and adults were consuming their picnic lunches or sleeping in the sun.

At the south end of Kilby Park, the Harrison River narrows considerably as it slides under the Canadian Pacific Railroad's trestle. People who don't enjoy listening to loud, rattling, clanging, banging freight trains on noisy metal bridges may experience difficulty in sleeping at Kilby Campground. The main line passes through here, and the metallic, clanking noises are heard at frequent intervals night and day.

There is plenty of fine trout-fishing water both above and below the railroad bridge. Immediately downriver from the trestle, where the river has narrowed and the current speed has increased, anglers fishing from the bank with light spinning tackle can cover most of the good fish-holding spots.

The coastal cutthroat trout, with its silvery, olive-gold-tinted body, its dense black spotting and red-orange slashes under its lower jaw, is the Pacific Coast's true native trout. Thanks to regular plantings of hatchery cutthroat, the Harrison has been able, to some extent, to

Two Dolly Varden (above) and one cutthroat trout (below).

Storm clouds at Kilby Beach, Harrison Mills.

Fly fisher on Harrison River.

uphold its historic reputation as a fine trout-fishing river, where anglers occasionally catch eighteen- to twenty-inchers. But these large specimens are exceptional, and rarely seen. Harrison cutthroat commonly run between nine and fifteen inches in length.

Autumn, when the salmon are running, is a good time for trout fishing, with October and November being the preferred months. Springtime also offers good trouting, particularly in March and April and there's always a chance you'll find cutthroat in the Harrison in late February.

In July, the waters of the Harrison River can drop quickly, resulting in some great trout fishing. Riffles and back eddies can produce well, and cover created by fallen trees or stumps can be a good bet. For the cutthroat trout try roe, egg sacks, worms, or spoons and spinners.

To me the Harrison is a cutthroat fisher's river, but cutthroat aren't the only game fish in this steam. There are white sturgeon, mountain whitefish, coho salmon, chinook salmon, Dolly Varden char and some steelhead. Not really renowned as a steelhead stream, the Harrison does give up some of these great game fish to anglers in the lower reaches. Many of these steelhead are bound for the Chehalis River, and a few of these Chehalis natives are intercepted before they enter the mouth of the Harrison's largest tributary.

*Above:* Harrison River at Kilby.

*Right:* Springtime trout fishing at Harrison River at Kilby.

A particularly prolific little fellow, the mountain whitefish is caught in the Harrison River in late winter and early spring, usually on small natural baits—maggots or single salmon eggs—but I have hooked many of them on wet flies and garden worms.

September to November is salmon fishing time. Fly fishers looking for coho will find the easily-accessed water near the highway bridge conducive to comfortable casting, while wading casters will appreciate the lack of steep banks and streamside bushes. Chinook migrate up the Harrison, but anglers must be sure to study the current fishing regulations for restrictions on these big salmon.

Here is an unusual fishery for fly casters. In Harrison Lake (headwaters of the Harrison River) there is some great fly fishing for trout and Dollies at the mouths of hundreds of creeks in the springtime. These game fish are feasting on young salmon fry emerging from the spawning beds and entering the big lake. Ask local guides and tackle shops for details.

White sturgeon that can live for a hundred years and reach lengths of over ten feet dwell in the Harrison River and in Harrison Lake. A first-time sturgeon angler would be well advised to engage a qualified professional guide, because sturgeon fishing is an extremely specialized sport, and I believe the sturgeon-fishing guide will insist that your chances of hooking sturgeon are better in the nearby Fraser River than in the Harrison.

Some sturgeon anglers prefer to fish for these leviathans at night. On a dark, warm, summer evening when we were camping at Kilby, Pauline and I visited with two nighttime sturgeon fishermen who were relaxing in lawn chairs at the river's edge and baiting their hooks by lantern light. I was fortunate enough to grab a fairly good flash picture of the nocturnal anglers as they watched their rod tips—by lamplight—for any possible indication of a bite.

The Harrison Valley lies in mountainous country. Big, rugged, wild, white frosted peaks seem to surround the twelve-mile-long Harrison River. The most striking, most easily recognized peak of them all is majestic Mount Cheam, across the Fraser River, to the southeast of Harrison. Cheam (pronounced "chee-am") is the "mountain of the snow angel," so named because the snow atop Mount Cheam lies in the shape of a white angel. Indian legend says that in the winter, if there isn't enough snow to form the angel, the salmon fishing will be poor in the Harrison. No angel, no fish.

# What's where ?
## And where is what ?

## Gamefish Species

Cutthroat trout, Dolly Varden char, mountain whitefish, white sturgeon, coho, chinook, chum, pink and sockeye salmon.

## Fishing Regulations & Restrictions

- **Cutthroat/Dolly Varden:** 2 per day, but only one over 50 cm.
- **Steelhead:** 2 hatchery steelhead over 50 cm.
- **Whitefish:** 15 per day.
- **Sturgeon:** catch and release carefully.
- **Coho salmon:** open Sept. 1 to March 31. (2 fin-clipped hatchery coho per day)
- **Chinook salmon:** total catch and release.
- **Chum salmon:** open year round, 2 per day.
- **Pink salmon and sockeye salmon:** there may possibly be openings.

Phone toll free: 1-877-320-3467, or visit DFO website www.pac.dfo-mpo.gc.ca

## Flies, Lures & Baits

Single barbless hooks must be used.

- **Flies For Cutthroat Trout:** Mickey Finn, gammarus shrimp, Mikaluk sedge, tied-down minnow, silver minnow and about two thousand other patterns.
- **Flies for Steelhead:** Umpqua Special, Davie Street Hooker, Cowichan Special, Art Lingren's General Practitioner (black) and endless others.
- **Flies For Coho Salmon:** Coho Sunset, Clouser Minnow, Pearl Mickey Finn, Chartreuse Popsicle, Coho Blue, Cathy's Coat.

- **Flies for Chum Salmon:** Popsicle Leech (chartreuse & Kelly Green), Harry Penner's Pink Fly, and most bright simple-pattern salmon flies.

- **Cutthroat Trout Lures:** Small weighted-body spinners, Flatfish and similar plugs (small sizes), small Five of Diamonds spoons, small Krocodile spoons and similar wobbling spoons. These lures, and similar ones, will attract Dolly Varden char and steelhead in addition to cutthrout.

- **Salmon Lures:** Kitimat spoons, Koho spoons, Hottentot plugs, Wiggle Wart plugs, Krocodile spoons, Spin-n-Glo Drift lures, Five of Diamonds spoons.

- **Steelhead Lures:** Medium-small-sized. Krocodile spoons, Five of Diamonds spoons, Spin-n-Glo Drift lures, Tee-spoons, salmon egg cluster imitations, and dozens of other artificial lures you can find in coastal BC tackle shops.

## Fishing Guides

**Harrison Bay Guided Services**
140 Esplanade, Box 65,
Harrison Hot Springs, BC V0M 1K0
Tony Nootebos, phone (604) 312-8070

**Gill's Fishing Tackle**
No. 4, 19300 No. 10 Highway (Langley Bypass)
Surrey, BC V3S 6K2
Brent Gill, river fishing guide for Harrison
Chehalis and Fraser rivers
Phone (604) 530-6266, Toll free (866) 530-6266

## Accommodations

**Kilby Provincial Park Campground** at Harrison Mills.
Phone (604) 824-2300

21 campsites. Wide sandy beach. Boat launch. Fishing in Harrison River. Open year-round.

**Glencoe Motel & RV Park**
259 Hot Springs Road
Phone (604) 796-2574

**Rainbow's End Camping Resort**
606 Hot Springs Road
Phone (604) 796-9417
$18 per day. Open March 1 to October 31.

# Distances to Harrison River

**From:**

- Vancouver, BC — 122 kilometers (76 miles)
- Blaine, WA, USA border — 114 km (71 miles)
- Calgary, AB — 785 km (487 miles)
- Edmonton, AB — 1031 km (640 miles)

CHAPTER **16**

# The Sasquatches of Chehalis

*God does not subtract from a man's life the days he spends fishing.*

— OLD PROVERB

The great hairy Sasquatch is alive and well, and is living in the mountains of the Chehalis Valley.

Many eye-witness accounts of sightings and other almost-irrefutable evidence indicate that the eleven-foot-tall mountain men known as Sasquatches are indeed residing in the Chehalis area, about eighty miles east of Vancouver, British Columbia. In the face of semi-documented proof, it seems evident that all the imaginative tales about the big Yeti or Abominable Snowmen in the Himalayas and the tall, hairy-bodied Bigfoot giants of Willow Creek, California, should be relegated to the category of myth, fairy tale, hoax or science fiction.

In my humble unscientific opinion the only genuine hairy mountain giants on earth are living in the Chehalis Valley of British Columbia.

The great Sasquatch mountain men have been an important part of Chehalis Indian folklore since time immemorial. Here are a few random samples of the accumulated documentation that prove, at least to me, that the Chehalis region is the true home of the Sasquatch:

In the mid-1880s, Alexander C. Anderson of the Hudson's Bay Company reported that he and his party were bombarded with boulders thrown by a hairy giant while they were exploring the Chehalis-Harrison area. In 1880, a young Chehalis Indian lady named

Winter steelheader on the Chehalis River.

Seraphine Leon disappeared for a year. When she returned home, she swore she had been kidnapped by a Sasquatch who held her captive in a cave until she persuaded him to release her.

In 1904, three Chehalis men—Michael Peters, his father and a friend—were canoeing down the Chehalis River when all three of them saw a Sasquatch strolling along the riverbank. In 1910, Peter Williams and a chum spotted a gentleman Sasquatch with a lady friend near Chehalis village. And one night in March 1934, Frank Dan of Chehalis investigated his dog's persistent barking and found a tall, hairy, unattired man standing just outside his door.

In 1948, a Chehalis Indian lad named Henry Charlie was riding his bicycle along a road near Chehalis village when he was joined by a ten-foot-tall gorilla-like creature walking beside him. The young fellow pedaled as fast as he could but, with six-foot strides, the mountain giant stayed alongside him without even breaking into a run. As Henry neared his home, the athletic Sasquatch left the road and disappeared into the bush.

If you need more proof that the Chehalis Valley is indeed the true ancestral home of the Sasquatch, consider this: The word "Sasquatch" was a part of the Chehalis Indians' vocabulary long before anyone else on the planet ever heard of the name.

Road access to the Chehalis River is a piece of cake. The gravel-surfaced old Main Logging Road crosses the river below Chehalis Lake (the river's headwaters). This is a logging road and drivers must respect any precautionary warning signs. The lower river, with some excellent pools and runs, is accessed via the paved Morris Valley Road. With some help from the river's fish hatchery, this glorious, scenic stream supports a summer steelhead run and a winter run. The winter run usually shows up early in December and continues until March, with the prime months being February and March.

On the Chehalis, when the water is low and clear, anglers often find steelhead resting in the canyon pools above the Morris Valley Road. But in freezing weather, the canyon floor and the steep canyon walls become icy and slippery, making footing extremely slippery and hazardous. A much safer bet during freezing weather is the Hatchery Pool, reached by a trail that runs behind the fish hatchery. Several years ago, I met two anglers, John Azevedo and Brent Siemens, and shot a photo of John releasing a fifteen-pound wild steelhead. He also released a big cutthroat and a dark coho salmon. Brent had a ten-pound hatchery steelhead that he had nailed earlier in the day.

Steelheaders can enjoy some fine sport on the Chehalis in July. The summer-run steelhead arrive in July and continue to show up until mid-August. The low water of July is clear, and a light line is needed for reduced visibility.

A few miles above the hatchery pool, the Morris Valley Road crosses the stream. The bridge crossing is rather important to anglers, providing access to good fishing water both upriver and down. Below the bridge, the sparkling bright waters of some of the runs are ideal for wading and casting. There is an excellent run in front of the Pioneer Christian Camp, a few hundred yards downstream from the bridge. Near the bridge a road heads southward toward the confluence of the Chehalis and Harrison rivers, winding downhill past some attractive homes, tidy yards and cheerful summertime flower gardens in the village of the Chehalis Indian Reserve.

Directly above the Morris Valley Road Bridge there is a small riverside campground operated by the Forest Service. At this rustic campground in the warm July sun, I have seen summer steelhead anglers, wearing nothing but shorts and tennis shoes, wading and casting and very obviously enjoying the pleasant weather. Warm sunshine really can make fishing a pleasant experience. As day draws to a close, activity ceases. But the Chehalis River—unlike us human beings—doesn't slow down however, or stop, or sleep, but continues with the endless job of carrying water from the mountains to the river mouth and, eventually, to the western sea. When sun sets and evening draws a shade over the light of day, and tiny insects dance over the Chehalis' waters, the sound of the river seems to grow louder—and some of the stream's gentler runs, silent during daylight hours, commence to murmur softly to us in the darkness.

In the autumn, when the leaves of the deciduous trees are painted golden yellow, burnt orange and flame red, and the mallard ducks are preparing to fly south, the silver-bright coho salmon begin to enter the lower end of the river and move upstream to their spawning beds. October can be a good coho fishing month. In November there are more fish in the stream, but many of them are losing their silvery sheen and are becoming dull and dark.

However, even in January and February, some of the late-arriving cohos look fairly bright, but often turn dark when they are killed. I have watched these late-run cohos—some surprisingly clean—in large numbers, below the Morris Valley Bridge.

Coho salmon are taken on fresh or preserved salmon roe, dew worms, ghost shrimp, wobbling lures, weighted spinners, drift lures, wet flies, streamer flies and many, many other lures and baits. When fishing the river for coho salmon in the autumn, river fishers often hook into cutthroat trout, Dolly Varden char, chum salmon and chinook salmon.

The Chehalis supports two runs of chinook salmon (alias spring, king, quinnat, tyee). There is a summer run of chinooks with red meat,

*Above:* Chehalis River steelheader near hatchery.

*Right:* Brent Siemans of Coquitlam and John Azevedo of Vancouver with his first steelhead

and a winter run with white meat. At present, chinook salmon are closed to fishing but interested anglers should check with the Federal Department of Fisheries and Oceans for possible openings. Thanks to the highly successful Chehalis Fish Hatchery, there are gamefish in the river virtually all year-round. Therefore, finding fish in the stream is not a great challenge. But there is a challenge worthy of our most determined efforts—the challenge of finding a big hairy Sasquatch. I know I'll be keeping a sharp lookout for one of these hairy mountain men and, if I'm lucky, I may witness a spectacle like James Cranebrook saw. In 1938, James and three friends witnessed a wrestling match between a Sasquatch and an adult bear. James reported that the Sasquatch won the fight handily.

# What's where ?
## And where is what ?

## Fishing Regulations & Restrictions

- No fishing from Chehalis Lake downstream (a few miles) to main logging road bridge. Also closed to fishing below this bridge May 1 to 31.

- **Steelhead:** Possession limit is one hatchery steelhead per day (hatchery steelhead have the adipose fin clipped).

- **Cutthroat Trout & Dolly Varden, Combined:** 2 per day (only one over 50 cm) minimum length 30 cm.

- **Coho Salmon:** Open July 1 to March 31. Limit 4 hatchery fish per day.

- **Chum Salmon:** Nov. 1 to Nov. 30. Limit 2 per day.

- **Chinook, Pink & Sockeye:** Closed.

**For clarification of regulations and possible recent changes:**

- Phone BC Fish & Wildlife (604) 582-5200
- D.F.O. for salmon regulations clarification (604) 702-2278
- Salmon Update Line (604) 299-9000, ext. 3467.

# Lures, Flies and Baits

### Trout and Char
- Wet Flies: Montreal, Parmachene Belle, General Money No.2, McGinty, Royal Coachman, Scarlet Ibis, and hundreds of others.
- Baits: Salmon eggs, worms, ghost shrimp.

### Steelhead
- Flies: Lingren's Black Practitioner, Pynk Dynk, Olive Woolly Bugger, Umpqua Special, Dynamite Stick, Polar Peril, Orange General Practitioner, and an endless number of new, old, popular and almost-unknown patterns.
- Lures: Gooey Bobs, weighted spinners, Koho Spoons, Krocodile Spoons, 5 of Diamond spoons, Kitimat spoons.
- Baits: ghost shrimp, dew worms, salmon roe, egg sacks.

### Coho and Chum Salmon
- Lures: Krocodile spoons, Koho spoons, Five of Diamonds spoons
- Baits: Salmon eggs, Dew worms, shrimp balls, whole ghost shrimp.

## Fishing Guides

### Brent Gill — Gill's Fishing Tackle
No. 4, 19300 No. 10 Highway (Langley Bypass)
Surrey, BC V3S 6K2
Phone toll free (866) 530-6266 or (604) 530-6266

### Tony Nootebos — Harrison Bay Guided Services
140 Esplanade, Box 65
Harrison Hot Springs, BC V0M 1K0
Phone (604) 796-3345, cell phone (604) 312-8070
www.harrisonbay.com

### Steve Arcand, Fishing Guide
Phone (604) 530-4983

# Accommodations

### Chehalis River Forestry Campground
For trailers. campers. tents etc.

Situated in mature trees, with 40 campsites, bordering the Chehalis River. Also two smaller sites across the road. Access by paved road.

### Kilby Provincial Park at Harrison Mills
Year-round. Birdwatchers! Bald eagles and swans here in autumn.
Phone (604) 824-2300

# Highway Distances to Chehalis River

**From:**

- Vancouver, BC — 123 km (76 miles)
- Blaine, WA, USA border — 114 km (71 miles)
- Calgary, AB — 780 km (484 miles)
- Edmonton, AB — 1025 km (637 miles)

# Index

Western Forest Products Ltd., 142, 146
Westwind RV Park, 60
White, Jack, 169
whitefish, 56–58, 66, 68, 88, 90, 171, 173, 200
whitefish, mountain, 15, 50, 54, 68, 94, 169, 172–174, 176, 197, 199–200
Wiens, Dave, 43, 46
Wigwam River, 175
wilderness campground, 36, 128
Williams, Don, 29
Williams, Peter, 204
Williams Lake, BC, 97, 99
windsurf, 193

wolverine, 81
Wolverine River, 59
Wycliffe, BC, 179

## Y
Yale, BC, 192
Yellowstone River, 89
Young, Bud, 145
Yukon, 39, 45, 54, 64

## Z
Zern, Ed, 180
Zuffa, Terry and Mrs. Zuffa, 171, 173
Zymagolitz River, 28
Zymoetz River, 28

# More Great
# HANCOCK HOUSE
# Fishing Titles

## The Master Angler
**Using Color
Technology to
Catch More Fish**
*Phil Rabideau*
ISBN 0-88839-561-2
5½ x 8½, 96 pp.

**12 Basic Skills of
Fly Fishing**
*Ted Peck &
Ed Rychkun*
ISBN 0-88839-392-X
5½ x 8½, 40 pp.

**195 Lakes of the
Fraser Valley Vol. I**
*Ed Rychkun*
ISBN 0-88839-339-3
5½ x 8½, 238 pp.

**195 Lakes of the
Fraser Valley Vol. II**
*Ed Rychkun*
ISBN 0-88839-377-6
5½ x 8½, 272 pp.

**Fly Fishing**
The Thornton
Anthology
*Barry M. Thornton*
ISBN 0-88839-426-8
5½ x 8½, 191 pp.

**How To Catch
Really Big Fish**
*Tara Robinson*
ISBN 0-88839-967-7
5½ x 8½, 64 pp.

**The Last Cast**
*Rafe Mair*
ISBN 0-88839-346-6
5½ x 8½, 128 pp.

**Mooching:
The Salmon
Fisherman's Bible**
*David Nuttall*
ISBN 0-88839-097-1
5½ x 8½, 184 pp.

**Pacific Salmon**
From Egg to Exit
*Gordon Bell*
ISBN 0-88839-379-2
5½ x 8½, 128 pp.

**Salgair**
A Steelhead Odyssey
*Barry M. Thornton*
ISBN 0-88839-412-8
5½ x 8½, 96 pp.

**Saltwater Fly Fishing
for Pacific Salmon**
*Barry M. Thornton*
ISBN 0-88839-268-0
5½ x 8½, 176 pp.

**Steelhead**
*Barry M. Thornton*
ISBN 0-88839-370-9
5½ x 8½, 192 pp.

**Trout Fishing**
*Ed Rychkun*
ISBN 0-88839-338-5
5½ x 8½, 120 pp.

**West Coast Fly Fisher**
*Compiled by
Mark Pendlington*
ISBN 0-88839-440-3
5½ x 8½, 152 pp.

**West Coast
Steelheader**
*Compiled by
Mark Pendlington*
ISBN 0-88839-459-4
5½ x 8½, 96 pp.

View all HANCOCK HOUSE titles at **www.hancockhouse.com**